THE
# FENG SHUI HOUSE BOOK
### CHANGE YOUR HOME, TRANSFORM YOUR LIFE

**GINA LAZENBY** *FOREWORD BY* **WILLIAM SPEAR**

WATSON-GUPTILL PUBLICATIONS/NEW YORK

*To Barbara and Geoffrey, my beloved parents, for teaching me to appreciate home and who have worked so hard through the years to help me keep my house in order.*

**First published in the United States in 1998 by Watson-Guptill Publications, a division of BPI Communications, Inc., 1515 Broadway, New York, N.Y. 10036**

Editorial Director **Suzannah Gough**
Senior Managing Editors **Jenna Jarman, Gillian Haslam**
Editors **Sarah Sears, Emma Callery**
Art Editor **Karen Bowen**
Picture Research **Jessica Walton**
Special photography by **Bill Batten**
Stylist **Arabella McNie**
Production **Julian Deeming**

*Library of Congress Catalog Card Number: 97-62240*

*ISBN 0-8230-1654-4*

*First published in the United Kingdom in 1998 by Conran Octopus Limited, 2-4, Heron Quays, London E14 4JP a part of Octopus Publishing Group*
**Printed in China**

*First printing, 1998*

*5 6 7 8 9/06 05 04 03 02 01 00 99*

# CONTENTS

# FOREWORD

## by WILLIAM SPEAR

Most of what is important to people has been all but lost in this fast-paced modern world. Beauty, truth, faith and nature are challenged every day by the constant assault of the nightly news, ethnic clashes, increasing pollution and degenerating health. Many feel that only their homes are safe – their only refuge, haven, ashram. But bringing what matters into our homes requires more than just a good decorator.

Much has been written and more will be debated about the immense changes we are experiencing in the design of our homes. But what universal principles apply, what timeless ways of seeing ourselves in relation to our homes exist in our history? What ideas and practices can make more difference than just a fresh coat of paint?

Creativity is a magnificent expression of our unique nature. So often a writer or painter is compared to another. All the time, the artist is, of course, searching for that special connection which distinguishes the work as original. This book comes not from arranging old ideas, but from creating emptiness first. When there is empty space in our minds, creativity fills it up. When a writer or artist clears out clutter, a hidden jewel is revealed. In interior design, few original creative expressions emerge which carry the impact of what you are about to read. Have no doubt – Gina Lazenby is one of a kind.

*The Feng Shui House Book* is about each individual in relationship to space. What is essential to understand is made perfectly clear in this beautiful volume: the spaces in which we live are both external and internal. We live not only in our bedrooms and kitchens but in our minds and the infinite space of conscious awareness.

This book will remind you of what you already know and will return you to true interior design. It affirms that lasting change begins from inside, deep within our souls. While this book may not at first strike you as a work of extraordinary personal transformation, let the reader beware! It is a book of philosophical importance like few others in this field, and Gina Lazenby's superb skill in presenting this material will change your life forever. As my student, colleague and friend, she has unleashed a clear self-expression and creativity which are inseparable from her commitment to personal transformation. The result of her dedication in this field has earned her great respect – not only for her work in public relations, organization and education, but now as a writer and teacher. This book is a gift of elegant simplicity for all of us to savour.

You are now about to embark on a journey into the deep inner space of your consciousness, beliefs and personal awareness. The result may bring beauty back into your life, harmony to relationships and renewed faith in the subtle mystery of life. This is the essence of 'interior design'. May you enjoy the most Fortunate Blessings!

ABOVE Surround yourself with beautiful things that you love. Choose items with special meaning and bring them alive with fresh flowers and plants. Each time you look at them you will receive positive endorsements from your environment which will boost your energy – consciously and unconsciously. Conversely, clutter and reminders of jobs undone will constantly drain your energy.

RIGHT Everywhere you sit or rest has an effect on your energy – the longer you are there, the greater the impact. Creating a calm, nurturing environment for eating will affect how you receive nourishment from food. Simple surroundings are less distracting and allow you to focus on the enjoyment of the meal and the company. This room is not overly full of art and ornaments to draw attention away from the food. The circular table with the rounded decoration and light fitting above all create a focal point to gather people into the space. The fresh flowers make the room feel alive, as does the view out to the garden. Adding curtains to the French doors would make the room cosier if used in winter.

# INTRODUCTION

## *What is feng shui?*

Feng shui is about how the environments in which we live and work have an effect on our physical, emotional and spiritual well-being. Different places make us feel differently. The amount of natural light flooding in through the windows, the colour of the walls, the type of chairs, the style of pictures and ornaments, the presence or absence of living plants – each aspect affects our experience.

Feng shui is the study of the movement of energy and how it moves in patterns, affecting every aspect of our lives. Quantum physics confirms that everything is made up of energy. All physical matter, no matter how solid it feels, is, in fact, only energy vibrating. All around us, in the empty space that we cannot see, energy exists as well. Feng shui is concerned with this invisible world, for it is as important to our well-being as the world we can see with our eyes.

Imagine, for example, walking into a room after a fierce argument has taken place there. You can feel the tension, in fact you might say that you could 'cut the atmosphere with a knife' because there is a tangible feeling of something hanging there in space. Likewise, scientific equipment has now been developed to measure the smallest movement of energy: the lie detector can register the most imperceptible fluctuation in vibrations of energy movement in the body.

Feng shui helps us to understand that our homes are direct extensions of ourselves; they are mirrors reflecting who we are. The places in which we live carry evidence and symbols of our past experiences, thoughts and dreams, and if we want to change and improve the quality and direction of our lives we need to understand how everything around us interconnects. In order to create a new future and make the things happen that we most desire, we have to consider how these might be represented in our homes now. In this book, you will learn how changes to the interior design of your home will be echoed by changes that are made to your life. Different arrangements will affect the movement of energy in your home and workplace. These will, in turn, be reflected in changes in your wealth, health, happiness, opportunities, relationships and feelings of peace.

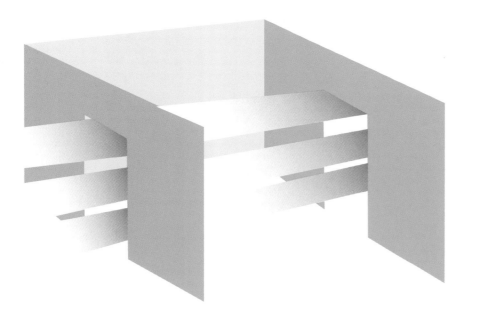

**LEFT** When two doors are lined up opposite each other, the chi energy moves through the room without stopping to nourish it. The room will not feel so comfortable and the area between the doors will feel like a corridor. If the front and back doors are opposite each other, the implications are more serious as good fortune and wealth come in through the front door, and are directed straight out the back. Slow down the flow of chi by placing one or two windchimes along the corridor's ceiling or place objects like plants on the floor.

**RIGHT** Rooms with just a single entry allow chi in and out through the same doorway or window as there are no other exits through which it can flow. This is good for creating a smooth, settling and restful energy in the room, but if the room is not used much, is blocked with too much furniture, or furniture is placed so that the flow is impeded, there could be stagnation.

**LEFT** Doors are like mouths and allow chi to be breathed into a space while windows are outlets for chi. The bigger the glass area, the more energy moves out and the more our attention is drawn from the room and into the outside world. You need to strike a balance between good views and being too open. Placing objects on the window ledge, like ornaments or plants, will help to hold energy in and draw attention to them before our gaze is diverted outside.

The goal of good feng shui is to arrange a space so that 'chi', or energy, can flow harmoniously so that it feels balanced. Energy moves in spirals and waves and we feel more comfortable when we emulate nature by bringing those same curves into our homes. Smooth and soft energy movement helps us to feel relaxed. Straight lines, angular corners and sharp edges do not mirror our own natural movement of chi, and so we can feel more stressed.

The relationship we have with a place is very personal as we bring our own unique character to it. Everybody expresses themselves in different ways with distinct preferences for colour, style, fabrics, art, and the nature and amount of their possessions. All these things create different atmospheres and have a different bearing on someone's life. So, although there are some basic principles to follow in feng shui, remember that having good feng shui is also about creating a home that reflects you and what you want. What has to be considered is what you want to use the space for, whether it is for bringing up a family, starting a new business from home, or beginning married life.

### *Where does feng shui come from?*

Like its name, much of the understanding of feng shui in the West today has come from the East, where it has been practised for thousands of years. The ancient Chinese had an understanding of the invisible world of energy that lay behind all things. Their knowledge and observations were expressed in the I Ching, a profound oracle which encoded, in its 64 hexagrams of broken and straight lines, a description of the nature of all things. This huge body of wisdom became the foundation of all traditional studies, including feng shui.

Yet the application of feng shui today need not be Oriental. Traditional peoples from all over the world have studied the relationship of humans living on earth under the influences of the forces of heaven. They have looked at the cycles of the seasons, the movements of the planets and, guided by their observations of the natural world, they have reached an understanding of the ways in which different places and homes can affect well-being and fortune.

Over time, different forms of feng shui have developed as practitioners recorded how they understood the nature of the world, classifying the information in maps and tables. Data on the shape and form of the land (Form School) and the charting of astrological influences on the Earth (Compass School) were gathered and evaluated.

Classical feng shui, which draws together aspects of both schools, is very much alive today because there is still a huge body of the oldest recorded information available from the Chinese. Whereas, originally, feng shui meant living intuitively through your heart and body, the classical approach was much more scientific and, with its complex calculations to evaluate the quality of the energy in an environment, was more about the mind. It has continued to have its appeal through the centuries. In this book, we look at how you can be guided by your intuition to determine what feels right for you

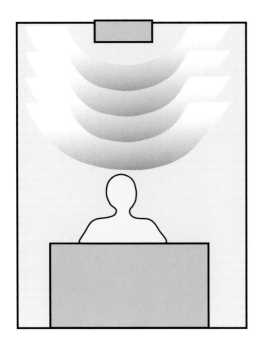

**ABOVE** Sitting at a desk or in a chair placed under a beam for long periods of time can be harmful. The smooth flow of energy above your head is interrupted and the waves bounce downwards, oscillating and affecting your energy field. Depending on your constitution, health and energy levels, this can have a debilitating effect over time. People who are more sensitive could get headaches, other people's immune systems may be subtly suppressed, while others will not be able to access their clear thinking when sitting under the influence of a downward force.

in your home. But it also actively presents a system of looking at how energy moves according to a 'bagua', a map of energy thousands of years old, taking into account the importance of symbolism, and understanding the relationship of everything in terms of five types of energy.

### Why are we interested in feng shui now?

Today, in the West, we have become a remote-controlled, instant, fast-food, push-button society, preoccupied by technological progress. We are becoming disconnected from the natural world, surrounding ourselves with much that is artificial, and exposing ourselves to increasing levels of toxicity and pollution in what we eat and what we bring into our homes. We are creating buildings that cannot breathe, which are surrounded by electro-magnetic radiation, with the result that our vital energy is becoming drained by what are now being called 'sick' buildings.

For all the advantages of modern, technological living, we have created a way of life grossly out of step with nature and without respect to the consequences our actions will have on the environment. Most of the lifestyle problems we face today were simply not around thousands of years ago. Electricity may feed us power but it robs us of our well-being when we unthinkingly live in its force-field. Geopathic stress is also more prevalent today because it comes from a distortion of natural radiation from the earth created by digging underground channels for water, communication and travel, and scarring the land with excavations for roads and buildings. We need to develop a greater awareness of what we have done and then take steps to compensate. There is a natural order in the universe of which our ancestors were aware – it provided a code for them to live by. No wonder there is an instinctive desire within us to return to a more natural way of living, to see how we can simplify our lives, without giving up the comforts of the twentieth century. Traditional lifestyles have much to teach us.

Research shows that our homes are less the entertainment centres that they were during the consumer boom of the 1980s. Values have changed. Refuge. Sanctuary. Safety. Calm. These are the key words that motivate us now, as we turn our homes into havens of peace where we can retreat from the outside world and screen all communications through our answering machines. People are now realizing that to create change in their lives they need to change their homes and it is this understanding of the link between us and our home that is at the heart of feng shui.

We have to de-clutter our spaces to create the physical space for energy to flow and for new possibilities to happen. Becoming aware of what we have around us, and the impact it has, allows us to make more conscious choices. In this way, we can learn to arrange our spaces to support our goals, whatever they are – to bring up a family in a stable and secure environment, to create a safe haven from which to explore the world, or simply to achieve peace of mind. This book marks the beginning of a new and exciting journey for you to look at your home in a different way, as part of your future.

**BELOW** Mirrors exert a strong influence. They affect you while you sleep, expanding energy in the room and bouncing it back to you. Meanwhile, your body is trying to rest, seeking repair and renewal. The brain sorts out information processed during the day and the body works on the damage we do to ourselves by eating processed foods and living in a world of mobile phone signals, microwave radiation and electro-magnetic stress. Mirrors sited opposite beds impede this process as the quality of rest is affected. Remove them or cover them up at night and your vitality in the morning will be markedly improved.

**ABOVE** Reflect your whole self and really get to know who you are. Mirrors in which you see yourself first thing in the morning and last thing at night can be most powerful. They reinforce our sense of self at those critical times when we are vulnerable, undressed and preparing for sleep or waking up to the world, moving into daytime reality from our dreams.

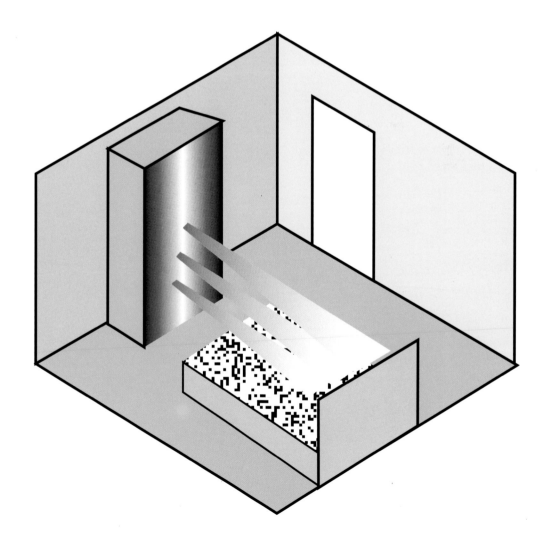

# BUILDING
*water earth thunder wind tai chi heaven lake mountain fire*
# BLOCKS

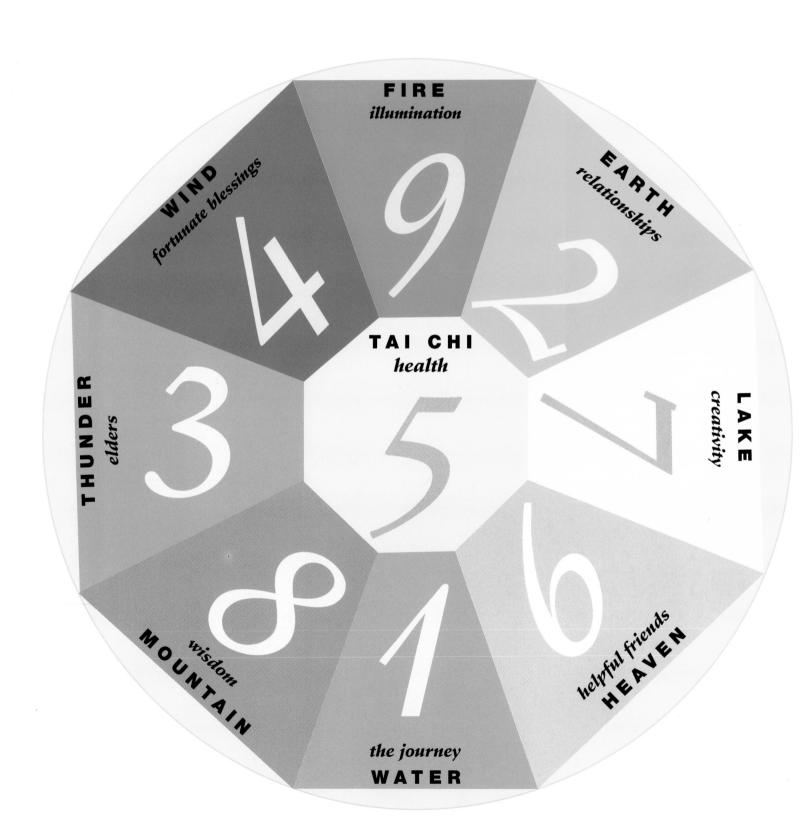

# THE BAGUA

*The bagua is a map of how energy moves within a defined space. It is a template divided into nine areas which can be laid over a plan of your plot of land, house, apartment – even the individual rooms.*

**LEFT  The bagua is an ancient map which shows how energy moves in the invisible world of vibration. An understanding of how it works will give you clues as to how you can create new possibilities in your life. It is a very powerful way of seeing to what degree your home is an expression of your life. Once you have placed the bagua on your home it will reveal what is happening for you at this moment.**

**If you live in a property that is evenly shaped and there are no missing areas or extensions, check out the different areas to see if there is something uncomfortable in the internal layout, decor or tidiness. Where there is a problem in the physical space, the bagua will guide you to evaluating the aspect of your life that correlates directly with it. For example, if an unused room is filled with junk waiting to be sorted and this room falls in Wind (4), your finances will likely have stagnated.**

**If you live in an apartment building, your bagua will start at your own front door, where your territory begins. If you rent a room, the bagua of the entire home will affect you. But the bagua for your own private room or area for which you pay rent will have the most influence over you.**

Each of the nine areas, or 'houses', of the bagua has a certain set of characteristics that gives clues to what is happening in your life and how this is mirrored in the shape and interior design of your home. There is a certain predictable pattern to the way energy moves around a space which has been observed over thousands of years. When the invisible energy moves into the area of the bagua known as Earth (2), for example, its impact in the physical world involves a relationship issue. In a similar way, any disturbances to the flow of energy in the area of Wind (4) will affect the inhabitant's fortune and finances. Each house of the bagua has many different qualities. It is named according to the trigram from the I Ching with which it is associated, and is given one of the first nine cardinal numbers.

The bagua is always orientated from the front door of your home or the main doorway into a room. Even if you rarely use your front door and always enter your house from the back, you should still use your front door to position the bagua; only use the other door as your 'front door' if you absolutely never open the acknowledged one. Using the grid of magic numbers that comprise the bagua (shown opposite), line up the template on your floor plan so that your door enters through the grid somewhere along the areas 8, 1 or 6.

Although the bagua is most powerful for the ground-floor layout of a building, each storey has its own bagua, which is aligned by using the top step onto the landing as the 'front door', and then pulling back the edge of the bagua to the outside wall of your home. Remember, too, that you can apply the bagua to any room in your house and also that doorways without doors can also be entrances. Sometimes, a room will have more than one entrance; as a crossroads room it could have three or four. You should align the bottom of the bagua with the doorway most frequently used: the door leading from the kitchen to the dining room might take precedence over the one from the living room, for example.

When evaluating your home, place the bagua over the ground-floor plan of the house to see if there are any sections missing, and think about the correlations there are with what is going on in your life. If the whole Relationships/Earth (2) area is missing, have you been finding difficulty with this aspect of your life? When you eventually start to think about making adjustments to the interior design of your home in order to begin to make changes in your life, use the bagua for each room. Consequently, if you decide you want to enhance your creativity, check each Lake (7) area of every room as well as on every storey of the house.

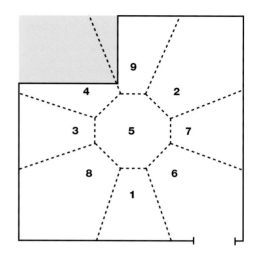

The bagua can be stretched to cover oblong and awkward shapes. As you lay the bagua over your own floor plan, you will begin to get an idea of what is missing, that is, what is called negative space, and what is an extension. Generally speaking, if the extension takes up more than half of the area from where it protrudes, then it is considered negative space. If it is less than half, then it is counted as a protrusion, which means that the prevailing energy of that house of the bagua is greater. Bay windows count as small projections.

Irregularly shaped houses with spaces missing should not be viewed as bad or difficult; rather, when you see the adjustments that you can make for each of the nine houses, you will realize that they have tremendous potential.

### *Feng shui questionnaire*

'If it ain't broke, don't fix it.' The purpose of the questions on the following pages is to guide you into making connections between aspects of your life that are less than satisfactory and parts of your home that could be changed. If everything is working for you, then it would be unwise to upset your life by starting to move things, just because this book might indicate that you should do so. Your home acts as your mirror; it is simply an extension of you and what is going on, or not going on, in your life. On pages 20–37, each of the nine houses is examined, with questions relating to each area of your life. Take time to answer the questions and note your responses on a piece of paper, giving each a score out of ten, noting the first number that comes in to your head – your immediate responses are likely to be the most accurate. Ten would mean wonderful and one would mean great dissatisfaction. Make a note of any adjectives and phrases like 'feeling stifled and blocked' or 'have come to a dead end', and then you can look around and see where these metaphors might be physically expressed in your home.

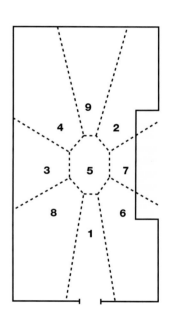

These questions will form the basis of any changes you might make in your home. The scores will allow you to prioritize where you start to make changes: choose the two or three lowest scores to work on first. Lower scores may reflect the fact that an area of your home is missing from the bagua – a negative space. Make each of the necessary adjustments according to how the energy needs to be nourished. Take it steadily and don't make any changes unless they feel truly comfortable to you. Once you have made adjustments, see if the room feels better. Then, if nothing new happens in your life within a month or so, come back to the book for further inspiration and try another approach.

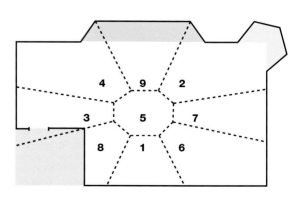

**LEFT** None of these properties are problem houses simply because they have pieces missing. In fact, it is much more interesting to live in such a place as there is more potential for change and for scope with interesting interior design. The first illustration shows a house with negative space in the house of Wind/Fortunate Blessings (4). People who live here will have a deficiency of energy in the aspect of their lives known as Fortunate Blessings, which could result in less opportunity and money coming their way.

Corrections here do not involve building an extension, which is good news for those living in high-rise apartments. Instead, the goal is to stimulate the movement of energy and this can be done with plants, lighting or a mirror on the internal wall, bringing the 'empty' room into the building. An illusion of extra space creates more energy. A small amount of energy is also missing from the house of Fire/Illumination (9) and any corrections will stimulate this, too.

The bagua is very malleable and can be stretched over long buildings, as in the second illustration. This also shows negative space in Lake/Creativity (7). Stimulating the energy around this part of the home would involve placements of soil and metal elements (see pages 40–41).

The third drawing shows both extensions in Earth/Relationships (2) and Fire/ Illumination (9), as well as negative space in Mountain/Wisdom (8). If the area of Mountain falls in the garden, enhancements could be made outside instead of inside. Exterior lighting, a bird bath and attractive plants and shrubs would all stimulate the energy of wisdom for the household.

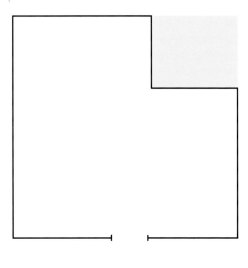

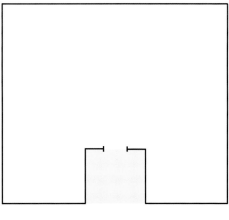

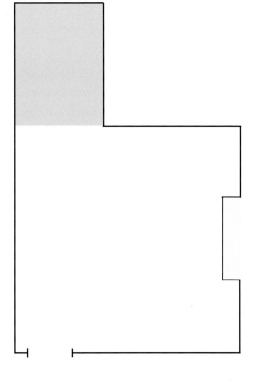

**LEFT** This first home shows a missing area in Earth/Relationships (2), indicating a deficiency in energy for relationships. Potentially, this house is more difficult for women to live in since the energy that is missing is from the most feminine house of the bagua. Relationships would also be difficult here, unless something is done to correct it – see page 24 for adding objects and colours which represent earth. The relationship corner of every room in the house could also be enhanced to compensate for this missing area.

The Water/Journey (1) area is missing in the second home, which does not bode well for successful careers. If this area is a courtyard outside the house, enhancements with plants and lighting could be made to this entrance area to bring it into the home.

The third home has a very large projection in Wind/Fortunate Blessings (4) which will amplify the energy of wealth and opportunity for the occupants.

The fourth home has an extension in the area of Fire/Illumination (9), so its occupants can be well-known or even notorious, depending on what they are involved in.

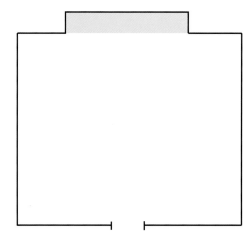

# THE NINE HOUSES OF THE BAGUA

The first house of the bagua is Water, which represents our movement through life and reminds us from where we have come, so it is more commonly called the Journey area. It is concerned not only with our career and the profession we have now, but the bigger issue of why we are here in the world. Are we doing what we really want or are we just earning a living? The way that chi moves through the world is like flowing water, so that when life is going well for us, we can think of ourselves as 'going with the flow'.

The house of Water is associated with willpower and drive. Because it is connected with the direction of north, it is cold and dark. It represents communication, emotions and discovery.

If this area is physically missing from your home then you will find it more difficult to get onto your path. Occupants of such houses will have problems with drive and ambition; possibly there will be confusion with communication issues. You can correct this by introducing the water element – either in the shape of a fishtank or mere images of water. Choose pictures that show some movement, which help to reconnect you with your right path; pictures of still water will, in time, lead to stagnation. Choose pictures that represent what you want to do or, if you have no idea yet what that might be, something depicting roads, routes or historical maps will act as a symbol to help you find your way. The colour blue can be used to nourish. A projection on your home in this part of the bagua will mean extra energy and focus to help you find what you really want to do in life.

Having a staircase here is not ideal because the energy is moving up and down too much; the energy of water needs to be more floating. If the entrance hall falls in this house, do you have more than one door that you can go through? Is this a mirror for where you are in life? Are you unable to choose a path? Keep the doors closed and open them only as you need to go through. If your hallway is outside your property but falls in the Journey – in an apartment building, for instance – decorate the external area with your own art and plants so it feels like your own space.

**WATER**
*the journey*

*Use the following questionnaires to evaluate your home. A lot of negative answers point to deficiency; if this area is not missing from your home it may be the barest place in every room.*

### Where are you now?

• Do you enjoy what you do?
• What is preventing you from moving forward to new things?

• Is your role in life fulfilling? If not, do you know what you want?

Take a close look at this area in your home. Is it cluttered and consequently blocked? Is this where the front door is? Does it provide easy access in and out of the house? Does your doorbell work properly? Are you available when opportunity calls?

Earth is the element of receptivity, openness and yielding. Energy here is manifested in the physical world in partnerships or, more generally, the Relationships area, so it is often called the marriage corner. If this area is missing in a house, it could be the reason why the occupant is single; couples living there are likely to have difficulties.

To maintain harmony and balance in relationships it is important to check out every relationship corner of the home to see whether negative space exists. The most important is the one in the bedroom since this is where you are most intimate in your relationship with yourself and with a partner. If the Relationships area is missing, you need to pay special attention to making adjustments. Moreover, as this house of the bagua carries the most feminine energy, a lack of this house can mean that female occupants will be less fortunate and happy. Make sure that this corner is not collecting clutter or housing an overflowing basket of dirty laundry. Check out the imagery of

*Where are you now?*

*•Are you happy in your relationship?*
*•Are you single with an active social life?*
*•Do you have a good rapport with your work colleagues?*
*•Do you feel isolated?*
*•Is your marriage going through a rough patch?*
*•Are you having poisonous arguments with your ex-partner?*

*If you give yourself a low score, check to see if the Relationships area is missing from your home or bedroom, or if it is cluttered and full of dead plants. Freshen up the area and introduce the symbols of soil energy. A small touch of red will introduce the element of fire and help to kindle passion.*

your pictures: are there solitary figures or couples having fun? Even a picture of two flowers reinforces the message of duality. Similarly, make the most of your relationships by showing mementoes of your life together. You need to energize the area, with up-lighting, plants, a crystal hanging in the window, a landscape painting with depth, or a mirror – whatever feels appropriate.

The nature of the element of Earth is one of openness and invitation. It is strengthened by flowing lines and soft items. Bring nature into your environment with flowers, plants, candles and water. Cushions and pillows on the bed are ideal reinforcements. The colour yellow holds the gathering nature of earth and can be used in the decor. Avoid furniture and decor that have a hard, unyielding quality. See where you can create welcoming corners that invite closeness and support togetherness – a window seat or a soft-covered pair of low, comfortable chairs facing each other.

*2* **EARTH**
*relationships*

# 3 THUNDER

*elders*

The third house of the bagua, Thunder, is associated with the family, elders and that which has come before us. In Eastern and traditional cultures older people are revered for their wisdom; indeed, they are often referred to as the 'long-living'. Their counsel is sought and they are shown great respect. We carry the spirit of our ancestors in our energy just as we carry their DNA in our genetic make-up and it is important for us to acknowledge our heritage. How can we know where we are going when we do not know from where we have come? Gratitude to our family needs to be expressed somewhere in our home; this area, most frequently referred to as Elders, is an ideal place for family photographs and treasured mementoes.

Stagnation in the form of clutter, things which you no longer use, or broken items in this area of your home may result in unresolved issues in your life and difficulty in starting anew. A lack of forgiveness on our part for some past misdemeanour or thoughtless act by an old friend or someone in our family can end up having a strong influence over our future. When we don't let go but hold on to the hurt it takes up space in our psyche and ends up holding us back from creating the future we want. This inability to let go is often mirrored in our surroundings when we hold on to old things from the past which serve no purpose now. A big clearing out of belongings, which you know deep-down you no longer need, can have a truly cathartic effect on your present and help to open up a new future. Lack of support from a strong Elders area will also affect your ability to be creative. Anything that symbolically represents difficulty from our past will affect the new future we are trying to create.

The shape of the trigram for Thunder from the I Ching has a solid line underneath which gives it a deep, base resonance, and indeed, it is associated with sound and noise-making. The energy of Thunder rising up in the east represents new beginnings, spring and the start of a new cycle. Thunder is associated with tree energy, which is represented by the colour green, tall shapes and plants. It signifies vitality and movement in the home.

As regards your home, a projection in this third house will mean a greater sense of maturity in the household. If the section is missing, occupants will lack energy and endurance, they may have to work harder, or find they have family problems. As this energy is connected with sound, where occupants are lethargic and stubborn, they can be shaken up and stimulated with the thunder of loud music flooding through the house. Noise-making machines like air-conditioners, hair-dryers, refrigerators, televisions and stereo systems all vibrate Thunder energy, and so does the human voice. Conversely, if you have problems with noisy neighbours, calm down the Thunder energy in your home. You can redirect this unwanted intrusion by a single tall plant to act as a channel for this strong energy. Reducing the colour yellow helps, too.

To correct an imbalance, you need to bring in the tree element – tall green plants, tall furniture and chairs, the colour green, artwork featuring green or woodlands or symbols of support, like pillars.

*Where are you now?*

•*How is your relationship with your family? Do you have good communication or family squabbles? Do you get on well with both your parents?*
•*If they have died, are there any unresolved matters lingering, or is there some resentment still bubbling away?*
•*Do you have family you can turn to for guidance in life?*
•*Do you find it difficult to get new projects going?*

*If you give yourself a low score, look at this area in your home. Is it missing or is this part of the house the junk room full of stagnant energy? Check out the Elders area in each room too.*

*Do you have any photographs of family groups, particularly ones where everyone is laughing and smiling? Or are all your family portraits of individuals, on their own? As this area is associated with tree energy, tall green plants are an ideal way of bringing harmony back into family relationships and generating the boost you need for new projects.*

# 4 WIND
## *fortunate blessings*

The house of Wind, or Fortunate Blessings, is to do with our experience of blessings and good fortune. Although the energy here does manifest itself in the world as money (which explains why it is often referred to as the 'wealth corner'), it is worth noting that our blessings often come to us in other currencies – opportunities, invitations, our children and friends.

The I Ching trigram for Wind carries the image of a flexible tree which bends in the wind. It represents growth, maturing, our sensitivity and assimilation of ideas brought to us like seeds on the winds of change. Because movement is associated with Wind, mobiles, fans and kinetic sculptures all stimulate Wind energy.

The energetic association with wealth means that having a bathroom and toilet in this area can be financially challenging. Energy is constantly being depleted by being dragged down the drains and basins, and the downward movement of energy when the toilet is flushed sucks away the positive chi energy which has gathered in your home, making it difficult for it to manifest itself as hard currency in your life. Take heart, there is a remedy that does not involve major replumbing. Healthy, upward growing plants, pictures of plants (for interior rooms without natural light) and small stones from a river bed acting as anchors can reverse the flow of chi. The toilet seat should be kept down at all times, plugs left in the drains and a small mirror hung on the outside of the bathroom door (which should also be kept closed).

When this area is missing in a house, accidents and misfortune generally follow. Adjustments involve tree energy again: plants and the colour green. And wood likes to be nourished by water, so this is an ideal place for an indoor fountain or fishtank. Pictures of moving water can also be used, for throughout time, water has been associated with life-giving properties, nourishment and the generation of wealth. If the missing area is contained in your garden, it is worth investing in exterior lighting, a bird bath and attractive plantings for even though it is outside, the space is activated by these, and positive energy is still generated. When there is a projection in this area, on the other hand, the household prospers and everything the inhabitants put their energy into will be more successful.

### *Where are you now?*

•*Do you feel blessed with what you have in life right now, however much or however little?*
•*Do you feel fortunate or do you feel dogged by bad luck?*
•*Have your bills increased since you moved into your current home?*

•*Do you have enough money? Or does it go as soon as it comes in?*

*If the area is not missing, see if your wealth is being drained by a bathroom. Do you have a lot of bathrooms, depleting your income? If the area is missing or dark, use lighting or a mirror to revitalize it.*

The fifth house lies in the centre of the bagua and although it does not have a trigram, it is strongly associated with Earth (2) and soil energy. It represents a unification of all forces and, as the key meeting point for all the energies, the Tai Chi is an important point of stability and balance, hence its more popular name of Health. This area of your home needs to be kept clear so that the flow of energy can pass through it freely. Clutter and stagnation here will have a great impact on all aspects of your life as it contains aspects of all the trigrams: whatever is present here will affect the stability of your life, health, relationships, family and plans.

This area is particularly important for your health, so keep it clean, tidy and uncluttered. Because real vitality and well-being can only be achieved if everything is in balance, make this space feel harmonious, using a good blend of all the elements and not just a predominance of one. You could reinforce the connection with Earth to act as a reminder to yourself to stay centred and grounded, which will strengthen your positive attitude to life. Introduce ceramics, empty containers and anything that is soft and receptive to help you to this end.

# 5 TAI CHI
## *health*

If this area is missing from your home, it can be a tremendous benefit. Indeed, traditional peoples would often leave an open courtyard in the centre of their house and use it as a garden, bringing elements of the outside world into the inside. At least two thirds of the space would still be clear rather than being entirely garden.

As this is an important gathering point and social centre, try to keep the middle of each room clear, particularly the living room. Do not block the central space by filling it with a coffee table; put that to one side to allow a better flow of energy and people.

***Where are you now?***

•*How is your health? Do you feel off-centre? Are you suffering ongoing problems or simply a general lack of energy and vitality?*

•*Do you feel generally unwell and in need of a tonic?*

•*Does your life feel crowded and overwhelming?*

•*Are you stressed? And do you feel burdened by the complexities of life? Does everything seem to be coming at you all the time?*

•*Do you feel the need to empty out and unburden yourself?*

Look closely at the area or room in the centre of your home. Is it a hub of activity with a free, uninterrupted flow of energy, or does it simply feel blocked and stagnant? Is it difficult to find any open space in your living room? Do you have clear and open areas for family and friends to gather in?

If any of these questions apply to you and your home, take a careful look to see if you can remove or rearrange obstructing furniture in this specific area in order to allow the passageways to 'breathe' again. You are likely to feel that the room, and as a consequence your life, opens up once again.

*Where are you now?*

- *Do you have a number of really good, close friends?*
- *Do you have anybody in your life who acts as a mentor or guide?*
- *Do you have friends who turn to you when they have real troubles?*
- *Do you have a network of support in times of crisis?*
- *Are you generous and supportive of charitable causes?*
- *Do you volunteer your time with any needy groups?*

*This corner of your room is great for photos of you enjoying yourself with friends. What have you got there now? Is it the barest part? Where is your telephone and address book? For a more active social life, place them in this area.*

*If you want to be more available to other people and want a stronger support network, energize this area with plants, lighting and metal energy expressed in round bowls and metal objects like picture frames. This area is also a good place to put pictures of angels or symbols of any other kind of helper that you want to attract into your life.*

Heaven represents the creative force of the universe and is the source of all things. It is associated with the archetype of the father – a figure of authority, strength, leadership, masculinity, achievement, awareness. Yet this house is more popularly known as Helpful Friends and represents all your visible and invisible means of support. Who do you rely on? Baby-sitters, people who run errands for you, and those who show up in your life like angels to get you out of a fix or as a shoulder to cry on. The force works both ways, however, so it also represents your spirit of philanthropy and your willingness to give of yourself to others.

This house is associated with the energy of metal, the colours white and silver, the season of autumn, and the northwest. It is represented by jewels, precious stones, crystals, symbols of masculinity and authority, legends, myths and stories.

If this area of your home is missing or lies in a built-in garage, you will miss out on the support of helpers and you will have difficulties with authority. As the energy here is the most masculine, men's fortunes and abilities will be undermined, children will not pay attention to their father, there could be upsets with male superiors at work, and men may spend more time away from home because there is less masculine energy resonating there. You can stimulate this energy by introducing metal, and nourish it with soil energy. Becoming a helpful person by doing voluntary work and making charitable donations can also help. The area of Heaven has a strong relationship with the house of Fortunate Blessings (4) in the opposite corner of the bagua. The more active this part of your home, then the greater the polarity between the two houses. This means that the more you give away of yourself in terms of philanthropy and time for others, the stronger the magnetism of Wind and the more Fortunate Blessings will come into your home and your life.

A projection in this area could mean that the household is very sociable and popular, with lots of comings and goings. As their energy is more strongly developed, male occupants would be favoured, and there is greater potential for them to be popular figures in the community but equally, with this emphasis on masculine authority, there might be an excess of male ego. Men may have a tendency to be dogmatic, while women are likely to feel less comfortable.

*6* **HEAVEN**
*helpful friends*

The nature of the seventh house is like that of the youngest daughter in a family: free-spirited, young at heart, full of hope and joy. It represents imagination and creativity, the senses and an appreciation of the arts, like music, dancing and painting. Anything that gives us pleasure – such as games, photographs, ornaments and prized possessions, – carries the essence of Lake.

Lake energy is synonymous with metal and is associated with romance, the late afternoon sunsets of the west, the golden glow in the sky and harvest. It is the time when we reap our rewards.

Deep within all of us is a longing to create, to leave something of value behind when we go, and it is particularly important for women to express themselves and feel creative in some way. For many, then, this something will be our children, but any project or business is just as much a product of our creativity. You do not need to be accomplished in the arts, nor do you have to write novels; it is enough simply to express your own unique inner voice without any fear of judgment – in whatever way is most appropriate for you. This could be cooking, arranging flowers or tinkering with cars. Holding Lake energy within can be damaging to your health, although problems in feeling creative or the ability to have children can also be linked to a deficiency in Elders (3).

**7 LAKE**
*creativity*

If this area of your home is too full or crowded, creativity can become stifled – just like trying to think when your mind is overloaded. We need to discard the old ideas that lurk in our heads and clear out the physical clutter from our homes in order to allow creative energy to flourish.

When this part of a house is missing, children are likely to be absent as well. There will also be a lack of pleasure, creativity will be a problem, and younger women in particular will have less supportive energy. Corrections might include introducing metal energy (white, metal objects and curves) and, in addition, supporting that energy with soil (yellow, ceramics and soft items). A projection in this particular area is likely to produce a more creative, more sociable household, which has a greater ability to make things materialize and to collect assets. Bringing things to fruition is synonymous with autumn.

***Where are you now?***

• *Do you have children? Do you want to have children?*
• *How creative are you? How do you express this creativity – in a social circle of friends, as an artist, musician or writer, through a business?*

• *Do you enjoy your free time?*
• *Do you have sufficient spare time?*

*Is this part of your home overcrowded or is there space for you to breathe? Check any deficiency in the Elders (3) area; unresolved issues can make creating a future more difficult.*

# MOUNTAIN
*wisdom*

The house of Mountain is about contemplation and inner knowledge, hence its more common name, Wisdom. Like the cave within the mountain, we need to be empty to receive wisdom rather than to simply fill ourselves up with knowledge. Mountain's qualities include heaviness, solidity, quietness and inertia. Objects that carry the nature of Mountain include containers, like vases, and heavy furniture, such as chests, cupboards and cabinets. A bedroom has a mountain quality because it is used like a cave, becoming a container for your energy while you sleep.

This immovable energy is linked with a great strength of will, the struggle to become established, and new beginnings, with effort being expended in achieving and being focused and single-minded. Earth is the physical opposite of Mountain in the bagua and so the relationships we have with ourselves and our inner world are extremely likely to have an effect on our relationships with others. So those wishing to strengthen their relationships, or find a partner and establish a relationship, need to reinforce this area, too. Mountain represents soil energy and is supported by items that

*Where are you now?*

•*Do you feel good about yourself?*
•*Do you have a feeling of inner peace?*
•*Do you feel stressed and disconnected?*
•*Are you able to detach yourself from the rush and bustle of the day and feel calm?*
•*Do you make time for yourself to tune into your inner wisdom?*
•*Do you cultivate your own Mountain time – how good are you at retreating in meditation or prayer, or for a long soak in the bath?*

*Is there somewhere in your home that you can retreat to – a place just to be? Sometimes we need to find a place somewhere that we stand still, like the mountain. The Mountain area is an ideal choice for reading or for storing your books.*

*When you strengthen the area of Mountain, you boost your sense of self. Do this with objects representing fire energy – red colours, lights and inspiring art. If you have an extension and find yourself involved in head-to-head arguments, drain the excess soil energy with metal objects.*

have a soil-like Mountain quality. It is also nourished by fire, which is represented by red, triangles, light, and anything that inspires, such as art.

A projection should be avoided if possible as this area needs symmetry and stability; a projection might create quarrels as couples will find themselves becoming increasingly separate in their opinions – like twin peaks of an immovable mountain. To rectify the potential problem, the excess soil energy needs to be drained by metal (such as white, curved, metal objects).

If the section is missing, the occupants will find it more difficult to feel peaceful and secure, and from such a base of instability it will be more difficult to create new beginnings. The mountain itself was formed by a rumbling energy in the earth, like a birth. As a result, if this eruption energy is missing in the home, occupants could find conceiving children extremely difficult; they may even have fertility problems. Moreover, as Mountain represents early nourishment, young children will also find it harder to be successful here.

# 9 FIRE
## *illumination*

The true nature of Fire illuminates the self and others, which is why this area of the bagua is most frequently known as Illumination. It represents clarity, vision, visibility and the eye, understanding and enlightenment. Its nature is expressed in light, candles and anything that has been created from inspiration or is likely to inspire us – sculpture, poetry, ceremonies and rituals, paintings by the great masters, classical music, treasures and sacred objects.

Fire's associated heat and incandescence gives it an explosive quality. The energy of Fire radiates in all directions and is like the peak of activity in the midday sun in summer. If you are not feeling inspired, maybe you are lacking Fire around you. If you have problems finalizing projects and feel unable to conclude anything, perhaps there is an excess of fire energy in your home – too much red or too many angular shapes. This fire is melting the energy of metal which helps you to complete projects and bring them to fruition.

Illumination means finding your way and this house of the bagua is directly opposite Water/the Journey (1), which is concerned with your path in life. The two houses – and their polarity in the north and south of the bagua – are about our sense of purpose and bringing vision into our life so that we can find that purpose, for it is much harder to steer a smooth course through the waters of life when Fire is deficient and clarity is lacking. If your career is in the doldrums, check the Fire area of your home as well as that of the house of the Journey.

If this area of your house is missing, poor eyesight may be an issue; there might be a lack of clarity, and problems with becoming well-known. A projection here is beneficial as regards greater fame and recognition but it may equally mean that dark secrets could come to light and bring notoriety with them.

### *Where are you now?*

•*Do you care what other people think about you or do you feel confident about who you are?*

•*Are you often easily swayed by the opinions of others?*

•*Do you feel that your reputation is important to you?*

•*Are you getting the recognition you would like or feel you deserve for your efforts in your work?*

•*Are you able to inspire friends and work colleagues?*

*Bringing clarity into your life may involve thoroughly clearing out the blockages found in the Fire area and then illuminating it with a mirror and additional lighting.*

*Our passionate nature and ability to inspire others may require the stimulation of the red of fire, but take great care with these placements so that you are not overdoing it. You don't want to go too far and provoke heated exchanges in the household, which can be the result of too much fire energy. Take it slowly and gently at first.*

# FIVE ENERGIES

*ABOVE Environments feel more harmonious when there is a balance of these five energies. We can create this by bringing in elements of each one. Here, tree energy is represented by the tall plant; fire energy in the lights, glass and touch of red; soil in the yellow and brown colours; metal in the use of the material for the lights, table and sofa base; and, finally, water through the floating shape of the sofa and irregular design of the lights.*

Everything in the universe is changing. To live more harmoniously with natural law, it helps to have an awareness about the patterns of change. These constant alterations of life can be seen in terms of five moving energies categorized as tree, fire, soil, metal and water. A basic key to understanding the practice of feng shui is comprehending that changes in nature are brought about by these energies. Central to Chinese thought, it was common practice to traditional peoples in the ancient world to consider these five energies as building blocks for every physical thing on earth. Furthermore, they have dozens of corresponding features which characterize all matter and the cycles of time. They help us to understand how energy moves and changes in the invisible world of vibration, which in turn governs how energy moves around our homes.

Because the strength of each energy affects the balance in an environment, knowledge of how each energy changes helps us to make appropriate adjustments in the interiors of our homes. There is a fixed order to the way they move and interact within a sequence that is continuous – with no beginning and no end. One cycle of interaction is the creative cycle which is nourishing and productive: for example, water nourishes tree energy and helps wood to grow, and in turn tree energy feeds fire. Another cycle is destructive, with one energy controlling another, weakening it and acting in an antagonistic way towards it. Fire energy melts metal, and as metal is symbolic of money, fire must be brought into and used in a room with care.

## *Tree*

The movement of the energy of tree is upward and outward and you would find symbols of it in your home in high ladderback-style chairs, panelling and furniture made from wood, upright furniture, tall plants and any painting with symbols of upward movement like tall trees. The nature of tree is associated with the compass direction of the east, new beginnings, the rising energy of a new day, springtime with all its fresh new life, the sunrise and the beginning of activity, and the colour green. Virtues of tree include patience, benevolence and endurance, while an imbalance can make people short-tempered and angry. A new project would benefit from a tall green plant; it would both successfully symbolize your new endeavour and support it.

In the bagua, the houses of Elders (3) and Fortunate Blessings (4) are symbolized by tree, so if you want to stimulate these areas, bring in more tree energy with symbols of wood, pictures of sunrises or tall plants. And as wood is nourished by water, supporting the tree with symbols of water energy (see page 41) would be a further enhancement. A kitchen would be well placed in the tree area of a home (the houses of 3 and 4) as this energy comes between water and fire in the creative cycle.

## *Fire*

The movement of fire is active and pulsating and it is associated with the colour red, pointed angles and triangular shapes – like flames. Fire energy is bright, like the midday sun, and is reminiscent of the peak of activity. It is associated in the bagua with the direction of south and the house of Illumination (9). It is represented by lighting, beautiful art, living things like animals, art that depicts animals and people, and angular-shaped furniture. It is also associated with chemical transformation and cooking, so the kitchen with its cooking 'fire' becomes the heart of the home. Virtues of fire energy include humour, reason, gentleness and being big-hearted. Too much fire can turn passion and excitement into panic and stress. Red candles and flowers on a dinner table can help to fan the flames of desire and create a romantic setting. The lively, active nature of fire also makes it ideal in a room used for living or social gatherings.

In the creative cycle, fire is nourished by the energy of tree: too little, and only a few embers burn; too much, and flames can rage out of control. You can stimulate the area of your home or any room that is associated with reputation and fame by bringing in fire shapes and red items. Nourish the fire with a few symbols of tree too.

*ABOVE Here is another environment where each of the five energies is blended well. Tree energy is strongly represented by the table, chair and tall flower arrangement; there is a touch of fire with the candle, cushion and photographs of people; soil is present in the yellow and in the long, low sofa; metal features on the table; while water is represented in the dark blue cushions and black-edged frame.*

**RIGHT** This diagram shows how the five energies move and relate to each other in the creative cycle. By having a full understanding of how each energy is represented in your home, you can easily change the feel of your environment. For example, by knowing that metal energy is more settling, you can bring in the symbols and colours of metal to a room where this feeling is more appropriate, like a dining room or a bedroom. By understanding that fire energy is very active you can use its symbols where stronger stimulation is appropriate – like a candlelit table for two. When you want to chill out and relax, create a more water environment with soft flowing lines and still, restful blue colours that are at the opposite end of the spectrum to get-up-and-go reds.

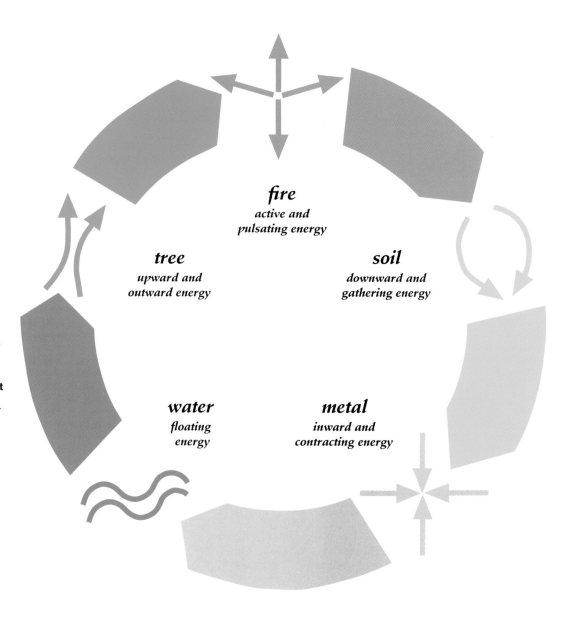

*fire*
*active and pulsating energy*

*soil*
*downward and gathering energy*

*tree*
*upward and outward energy*

*water*
*floating energy*

*metal*
*inward and contracting energy*

## Soil

The nature of the movement of soil is gathering and downward. It symbolizes the settling energy of the late afternoon, the ripening of the crops and gathering of the harvest, the process of maturation. Its colours are yellow and brown tones. Rather than being aligned to one of the four compass directions, its position is central, so it is very much associated with gathering things into the centre. It is allied with three houses of the bagua: Wisdom (8), Relationships (2) and Health (5). Soil virtues include honesty, sympathy, wisdom and consideration, so it has a supportive, receptive and nourishing quality. When it is out of balance, however, it produces scepticism and irritability.

Features in the home that represent soil energy include wide and low furniture, side tables, long comfortable sofas and big, soft cushions. Earthy materials like terracotta and ceramics are also linked to soil. A family gathering where it is important for you to bring everybody together would benefit from yellow flowers in a stone jug.

Soil is nourished by fire, so red symbols would also strengthen relationships. In turn, soil creates metal like the ore that is found in the earth, so anything of a soil nature would support the metal areas in the bagua. The gathering nature of soil makes it an ideal location for a dining room and its settling energy is also good for digestion.

## Metal

The nature of the movement of metal energy is inward and solidifying. It signifies a time at the end of the autumn when we enjoy the fruits of the gathered harvest, a time of reward, moving towards completion; it is aligned with the west with a view of the golden glow of the sunset. It is associated with two houses in the bagua – Helpful Friends (6) and Creativity (7).

The shape that represents metal energy is the circle, so buildings that have many curved features and arches have a metal nature. The use of metallic features like stainless steel and the colours white and gold also represent metal.

Metal virtues include righteousness, happiness, security and wholeness, but an imbalance prompts melancholy and sadness. Metal also represents the energy of money, cashflow and our ability to create tangible rewards and results from our efforts. Thus, a vase of white flowers in your study is helpful when you need to concentrate your mind and complete a task. In the creative cycle, metal is nourished by soil so Creativity, for example, would benefit from both soil and metal symbols. The descending and settling nature of metal makes it ideal for use as a bedroom or a study where you want to focus.

## Water

The energy of water is floating and still. It represents the quiet, the darkness of midnight, the stillness of winter. From this stillness and the depths of darkness we receive insights. Its associated colours are blue and black, and its shapes are irregular, asymmetrical, organic, free-flowing and even shapeless. It is associated in the bagua with the house of the Journey (1) and the north.

New ideas are generated when they come forth from the depths of our creativity. The virtues of water energy include confidence, courage and willpower and so, when water is out of balance, there are feelings of hopelessness and a total lack of self-esteem in our lives.

In the creative cycle, water is generated by the melting of metal energy. When it is important to reinforce the strength of water energy in a room or your home, place symbols of water or the colour blue there. Bringing in metal energy by adding white, round shapes and metal objects will give further nourishment. The still quality of water means that it lends itself as a good place for retreat and meditation, or as a storage room.

# DESIGN
# PRACTICE

storage  bright objects  sound  living objects  symbols  water  placement  colour  shape

# STORAGE

First let us consider the important difference between storage and clutter. Storage is neat, tidy, clean and accessible. It encompasses all the places where you are holding materials to use at some point in the near future: attics, basements, garages, sheds, wardrobes, display cabinets, underwear drawers, jewellery boxes, cabinets, spice racks and tool kits. Items being stored should be classified as being valuable, useful or treasured, or ideally all three. If you do not love something, or need it, then it has to be re-defined as clutter, and if we are honest, many homes are overflowing with too much clutter which is trying to masquerade as something useful.

Clutter includes the things which you are not using; the unwanted gifts you feel obliged to display; useful objects which have not got a specific home and are in the wrong place; unfinished jobs which gnaw away at you like half-finished knitting, heaps of half-read magazines or a month's pile of household mail.

All your storage places, such as overflowing wardrobes and overstuffed attics, are having an effect on you. Every time you open a door and see the chaos on the shelves behind it, you are being affected. It is giving off the wrong kind of energy and adding to the confusion in your life. You are connected to everything you have ever

*ABOVE When people moan about having nothing to wear, it is often because they cannot find suitable outfits. Storing different types of clothes by category in different shelf and rail sections really supports you and makes you feel more organized and in control. If your first view every morning is a chaotic wardrobe with shirts, socks and sweaters tumbling everywhere, then this will influence your mind for the rest of the day. Your world view of disorder and difficulty is constantly being reinforced by the muddle at home.*

*RIGHT There is a beautiful simplicity in this room where everything is stored away and all materials are natural. The horizontal lines of the bed and door balance the vertical lines of the door frame and wardrobe. This storage is much better than mirrored door fronts which are very disturbing to the quality of sleep. A simple and natural environment fosters a corresponding lifestyle.*

ABOVE While it is preferable to keep bedrooms clear of distractions, this occupant obviously does not like to be separated from favourite books, and at least the shelves are not full. The soft cloth in the doorway adds a contrasting lightness to the otherwise heavy, large books. It is also good to store lighter items like the baskets over a doorway.

TOP RIGHT If you provide good shelving and an ordered environment for children to store their books and toys you are encouraging them to take care of their belongings and be tidier. Create the structure and the processes will more naturally follow. Red tubing and yellow shelves makes this a fun place to hold a child's treasures.

ABOVE Crowded shelves reflect crowded lives. Many households have beloved collections of precious books, and people cannot bring themselves to part with a single volume. At least keep them dusted, review them from time to time and let some go, and ensure that they have breathing space by placing ornaments and pictures between them.

ABOVE  A simple yet beautiful environment, basic without any frills but nevertheless reassuring with the heavy wooden cabinet and neatly arranged chairs. There is just enough china here within easy reach of the table, and the cabinet doors mean that it can be hidden out of sight after the meal. At the end of a day that has been spent working in a frenetic environment with an overwhelming workload, this dining area must feel like a real sanctuary, nourishing the spirit as well as feeding the appetite.

RIGHT  The kitchen is the real heart of the home. If there is simplicity and clear organization in this room, then these same qualities will pervade through the food preparation and imbue the occupants of the household. Clean, clear, orderly storage of kitchen equipment not only inspires the cook to create delicious meals but ensures that calmness will be the order of the day. This is particularly important in kitchens that have open shelving. It is preferable to store sharp knives out of sight.

bought or taken possession of; you are developing some kind of emotional attachment, which is why it can be quite difficult to throw things away.

The more you have, the more it begins to drag you down so that it feels as if you are actually carrying around the weight of everything you own. Clutter impedes the smooth flow of energy around your home and therefore in your life. In the end, having too much becomes a drain on your energy, impeding your progress in life.

Look and see where your clutter is. How does it relate to the bagua? If you cannot open the front door because of the sheer quantity of boots and coats, and this is sitting in the career area of the bagua, it is easy to see why you might be having problems in finding the job you really want. The more difficult you make it for the energy to flow by creating stagnation with piles of magazines and books on the floor, the more you will create obstacles in your life. They will pull you down to the ground.

Your goal should be to surround yourself with healthy, vibrant and free-flowing chi energy. Anything which does not contribute to this is having an adverse effect on you and it has to change. It is very difficult to feel fresh and alive and full of vitality if you are surrounded by stagnation.

A whole book could be written based on the incredible stories told by people who have had a big clear out and seen their lives transformed. And if you are only inspired to do one thing as a result of reading this book, then let it be clearing out the clutter of things which are no longer useful to you. It will give you an amazing sense of release and freedom. Remember, if you want to create a new future, then create some space in your life for new possibilities and new opportunities to come in. Potential needs a little bit of breathing space! Do not, however, confuse clearing out clutter with making your home into a minimalist's dream. Just make sure that you only surround yourself with the things you really love and try to exercise some restraint from time to time by adopting the principle that less is more.

*TOP  Not everybody likes to live in a minimalist environment and some people feel reassured by having huge collections of things they love. A more cluttered look can work if part of the display is usable, like the jug holding the flowers, and provided it is moved around instead of becoming stagnant.*

*ABOVE  This plain and simple display has a different appeal to the one above, which is constantly entertaining the eye. The scalloped frill on the shelf shields the sharp edges.*

# BRIGHT OBJECTS

*ABOVE  Using light and glass is one of the simplest ways of activating chi energy in an area. Glass shelves in a window lift the energy much more than wooden ones, and with the addition of green and blue coloured glass bottles (the colours representing tree and water), they would be most appropriate for enhancing a wealth corner. A small, crystal sphere has also been hung in the window on a clear thread.*

*OPPOSITE RIGHT  The placement of a mirror over a fireplace creates a powerful focal point in the room, with the reflective silveriness of the mirror providing a cooling antidote to the heat of the fire. As this mirror will attract most attention in the room, be conscious of what the mirror is reflecting. If your room is cluttered, your mirror will certainly expand this and whatever difficulties you have will effectively be doubled. Mirrors in a living room can also be positioned to reflect the natural world outside into your home. Views of water are particularly healing.*

Bright objects are those with reflective qualities like glass, mirrors, crystals and anything with a shiny surface. They activate energy by attracting or magnifying light. Glass objects and ornaments, metal statues, gold-trimmed dishes, tapestries with metallic threads and sequins: all these things sparkle and glitter and enhance the level of chi wherever they are placed. They are especially useful in dark corners and plain, undecorated areas. Try putting something sparkly in the Helpful Friends (6) corner of your house or room and see what support suddenly appears out of nowhere at that precise moment when you really do need someone.

Light itself also adds brightness, and rooms will feel different according to the amount of natural light that is coming in and how artificial light is being used in the space. Light is energy. You can make dramatic changes to the mood and feel of a room by turning off a bright central light and switching on smaller lamps to illuminate dark corners and create low pools of light. By introducing light fixtures to appropriate places in a room, you can also activate particular areas of the bagua. A lamp is a good correction for negative space in the bagua. Uplighting will also help to lift the chi in a room where there are overhead beams, heavy furniture, or a low ceiling causing a downward movement of energy.

Clear, faceted crystals have an extraordinary capacity to activate energy. One small sphere hanging in a window can have a dramatic effect on a room, especially when it catches the sunlight, and it can add a powerful charge to a particular area of the bagua. Placed in the space corresponding to Fortunate Blessings (4), for example, it can have a positive impact on your finances. Crystals are also very effective hanging in the window that faces onto an area outside your house which represents a negative space in the bagua.

Mirrors are the most commonly used bright objects for improving the feng shui of a space. They are often called the aspirin of feng shui but they should be used with great care because they are extremely powerful at expanding energy and making space larger. Mirrors enable energy to flow in small, tight spaces such as in narrow hallways or through doorways which open right into a wall: imagine how claustrophobic you would feel in an aeroplane washroom if there were no mirrors to make the cubicle appear much larger. When the floor plan of a room or of a house has an area missing (see pages 18–19), mirrors are also ideal for creating the illusion of the space being there. By expanding the energy of a space you can bring additional impetus to that part of your life which corresponds with that space in the bagua. Place a mirror in your hall, for example, and if it corresponds with your career area, see what new opportunities begin to come your way.

TOP  *A chandelier uplifts energy and helps draw people together.*

ABOVE  *Here energy is being magnified by the beautiful cut glass bowls, vases and jugs. The facets of the glass-cutting create an additional sparkle.*

## TIPS FOR MIRRORS

• The hard edges of unframed mirrors can be unsettling so frame them or at least ensure the edges are bevelled.

• Shape can change the effect; round or oval mirrors are preferable for creating harmony in bedrooms and in small spaces such as bathrooms.

• Mirrors must be spotlessly clean and unbroken so that the reflection they give is a true one and not in any way tarnished or distorted. It is most important not to use antique mirrors that have become mottled over the years.

• The position of mirrored wardrobes in bedrooms can be a tricky issue. Avoid being able to see yourself reflected in the mirror as you lie in bed, as this will affect the quality of your sleep adversely. Mirrors expand energy, which is the opposite of what is happening in your body during the hours you spend asleep.

• Mirrored tiles can present real problems since they are literally slicing you up and can have a very disturbing effect, particularly in a living area.

• Make sure that what you are reflecting is positive. Bring in the elements of nature by showing the reflection of the trees outside, but be careful when the image is one of a cluttered shelf filled with all those things you do not want to be reminded of. The reflection will have the effect of doubling the negative qualities of a space.

*ABOVE  Just like magpies being attracted to bright objects, so our attention is caught by the sparkle from these silver balls, the glints of light reflected off the pearlized shell and the gleam of the glass goblets.*

*FAR LEFT  Mirrors are useful for expanding dark corners and for re-routing the flow of chi around tight spaces. They help to open up walkways and here they are positioned on either side of an opening between two rooms, making the space feel more like one area.*

*LEFT  The basic function of a mirror is to reflect the human image. We use them daily, particularly in bathrooms, and as it is the only time we can see who we are, it is important that the image is a true reflection. Pay attention to the clarity of the glass and ensure that the mirror is whole. Avoid placing two mirror sections side by side (as in some bathroom cabinets), as your reflection is split.*

# SOUND

The basic premise of feng shui is to create harmony in the home and to do this we need to do more than just think in terms of room design, furniture layout and colour schemes. Sound is an important part of our environment because of its ability to heal, inspire, energize and soothe our spirits. It can change the ambience of a place completely. First, you should examine all the unwanted sounds that your conscious mind may have already decided to blot out: the whining refrigerator, the clanging bathroom pipes, the humming air conditioning, the whirring central-heating pumps and the incessant drone of traffic from outside. These noises are a constant energy drain and can easily upset our nervous systems.

Beyond the obvious and mundane adjustments, such as removing or switching off non-essential electrical appliances, and ensuring that everything is properly installed and well maintained, you may be able to reduce their adverse effect by masking the sound with white noise. Uplifting or tranquil music or the sounds of nature can act as positive background sounds: a small indoor waterfall with its soothing sounds of running water, or a tape of birdsong or the oceans are each remarkably effective. To absorb some of the sharp, intrusive sounds of footsteps on a stone floor, introduce more wall hangings and green plants.

You can make subtle and powerful shifts in the energy of your home with sound-makers like windchimes and musical instruments. A windchime will moderate the flow of chi energy and its sound will alert you to the fact that you are moving from one environment to another as you walk from room to room, in the same way a bead curtain moves subtly in the current.

*LEFT Windchimes can be used in the doorways of, say, kitchens where the layout means you have to prepare food with your back to the door. One useful way of knowing when someone is entering the room is to place a windchime in the doorway. Another method is to hang a bead curtain that makes a gentle sound when pushed to one side. Whatever you use to mark the transition from one space to another, make sure the sound is gentle and avoid things with tones which jar the nerves like the strident buzzers found underneath shop doormats.*

*LEFT* Many people associate the placement of a windchime with making feng shui adjustments, but few understand what they actually do. In fact, they have many effects on our environment.

First, they help to define boundaries and mark the space between the indoors and outside through sound. The gentle tinkle of a chime will let you know that you have entered a different environment or moved into another room. They are good for marking the edge of your property and can be hung from a tree and not just an entrance doorway.

Second, they help to moderate the flow of fast-moving chi and can be hung indoors on the ceiling of a very long, straight corridor. As sound changes a mood it is important that you choose a windchime for its chime and not its look. Play several until you find one that seems just right and resonates with your own energy. It should be a very personal choice. Windchimes can be made from metal, bamboo or ceramic, and shaped as tubes or bells.

Sound is great for cleansing the air and shifting energies. Play some loud music just before you clean and it will help to lift a room, making it feel brighter.

ABOVE Plants provide natural protection from noise and air pollution and give great shading for very bright rooms. In conservatories, it is important to have large plants to keep the chi energy within the room, rather than allowing it to be drained away through the large panes of glass.

RIGHT Watch for where your cat or dog likes to be in your home with respect to the bagua. If your cat takes up residence in your bedroom or your dog favours your Relationships corner, you could end up missing out in your love life but have a great relationship with your pet.

# LIVING OBJECTS

All these cures and adjustments work on the chi energy that already exists in your home, by affecting its movement and/or its quality. Here we look at how you can actually increase this energy by introducing things like plants and animals which are alive. Living chi can make a dramatic improvement to a room which feels dull and stale.

The more time we spend indoors and the more synthetic our environments, the greater is the need to have plants, which will help to restore the equilibrium of energy. Because healthy plants are a potent source of chi to activate your life, you can position them in particular places in the bagua: your marriage or love life will definitely perk up if you put a strong, vibrant plant in an empty relationships corner. Where you want to introduce tree energy as an adjustment, use green plants, and particularly tall varieties that seem to embody energy moving upwards strongly.

The space agency NASA has researched plants to find the best ones for cleansing atmospheres. Spider plants, poinsettias and jade 'money' plants have been found to absorb more electro-magnetic radiation so they are ideal to place in rooms where you have electrical equipment. Avoid plants with sharp, pointed leaves, especially for small environments. Wide, rounded ones are better. Sitting next to a grand palm with the spiky ends aimed directly at you will make you feel uncomfortable; these plants need more space and are better suited to larger public places. Plants help to reduce stress and can provide protection by absorbing air-borne pollutants and toxins. Keep them healthy and replace them as soon as they are on the wane or they will drain the energy. It doesn't matter if you are not particularly good at tending them; the benefits of being supported by living chi will far outweigh the cost of constantly replacing them.

Plants rooted in soil help to ground and balance us, so having an indoor garden or conservatory in which to potter about, handling soil and watering plants can be immensely soothing, particularly if you do not have a garden. Good feng shui is about strengthening our connection to the natural world, and bringing nature indoors is an excellent way of doing this. Dried flowers have no life and should be used in your home in moderation. Change them frequently with the seasons rather than holding on to them for years, as they will hold stagnation.

Animals contribute to the life force of a home too. They move chi as they move around, make a place feel more lived in when you come home, and act as a focus for our love and attention. As a goldfish bowl holds water, it has an added bonus: water is good for healing and prosperity. Pictures of animals can be just as powerful; a room with several images of cats can make it feel as if the animal is really there and adds more energy to a space than, say, pictures of bowls of fruit. However you arrange your home, make sure that you are not the only living thing there.

*TOP Anything that moves will activate chi, so even though caged birds are not flying, their movements and their birdsong will enhance the energy level of your home. If you prefer, place a bird bath in the garden which will attract local birds and activate the energy around your home.*

*ABOVE Watch out for places where cats love to sleep as they are attracted to geopathic stress (see page 12). If you move your bed but the cat chooses not move with you, preferring to stay put in a particular spot, then it is highly likely that you have some negatives energies.*

*ABOVE This stairway has been transformed by the addition of three large scroll maps. They lift the energy up the stairs and act as constant reminders of places the occupant might wish to visit. The red drapes also act as effective brakes for the energy naturally moving down the stairs.*

*RIGHT Choose artwork and paintings that have special meaning and give you inspiration. If you are hankering to experience a country idyll, then a restful scene like this mural depicting a shepherd with his flock will feel appropriately soothing and make your dream more achievable.*

# SYMBOLS

Symbols are an important part of our everyday lives; they help us to make sense of the world. They are the language of the unconscious mind, and they are used very powerfully by the modern media to inform and persuade us. Fables, parables and stories have been used for millennia to help us understand ourselves, while icons, totems, talismans and lucky charms all potentially hold a special power or message. They may have the ability to influence consciously or unconsciously, but the more we understand them, the more control we have and the more we can actually use them to enrich our lives in whatever spot we choose.

Everything in our homes carries some significance as a symbol. Our home is an extension of who we are: we have chosen it, decorated it, and whether or not we realize it, we have filled it with things that have special meaning for us. This is a highly personal process, just like choosing the clothes we wear. Our homes become metaphors for our lives and simply reflect the issues that we are facing. You should not be surprised, for example, to find your career area completely bare at just the moment that you find yourself at a crossroads and do not know which direction to take with your life.

To understand how the relationship works you need to understand how the nine houses of the bagua are simply metaphors or symbols for how energy is moving in your home. Look at your floor plan. If it is not an exact square or rectangle, which section is missing? In what way does this relate to your life? Is your area of relationships missing and are you single? You will probably find that the messiest area of your home is the one which happens to match the aspect of life in which you have the most difficulty. An inability to clean up and create order is a symbol for your inner confusion.

Take a look at your home from a maintenance point of view. Water leaking away through broken pipes or damp patches will probably show up as red ink on your bank statements. Any doors to rooms or cupboards that require extra effort to open will signify some level of struggle in your life. Conversely, if cracks are starting to appear in your relationships, take a look at your ceilings. If you feel a bit cut off, and not part of a social circle, see whether there is an overgrown hedge obscuring your front door, acting as a barrier between you and the outside world.

Our homes are full of symbols which are constantly affecting our energy. The art we hang on our walls can be a potent source of inspiration. If we focus on something, it will attract energy and it will become a catalyst for synchronicity, starting to draw in the events and people which are necessary to make things happen to our lives. Hang pictures of places that you would like to visit in the future, and not just the places you have been to in the past. Watch out for the coincidences that will happen between when you place the picture and when you actually book the trip there.

*ABOVE Pathways represent our journey through life and as such it is better that they move in a curving, flowing way, reflecting life as it unfolds, rather than in a straight line and with sharp corners mirroring abrupt change. Laid out as individual stepping stones, paths also reflect how we move forward in stages.*

*ABOVE Single people who would rather be in a relationship are surprised when they realize that they have collected several images of people on their own. When you don't want a solitary life, choose artwork of couples, particularly for the bedroom.*

Hanging abstract art where you want clarity and focus could well leave you feeling fragmented and incomplete. Similarly, on a negative note, people who sometimes feel lonely will often have surrounded themselves with stark landscape paintings populated only by solitary figures. You should think twice before you hang that clever etching of a hillside in the driving rain; consider that you may well end up having to spend the money you are saving for a rainy day.

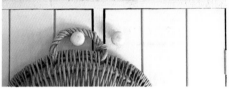

*LEFT Fish are associated with wealth, and often feng shui advice will urge you to place a fishtank in your wealth area. The link is strong, so placing wooden fish in this part of the bagua will also affect your finances. Numbers have a special significance, too, so avoid having three objects in your relationships corner; triangles are very uncomfortable.*

*RIGHT When you know you want to change your life and find your life's work, but you have no idea what that is, check out your career area. If it is empty, at least place an illustrative map in the area to help guide you through the transition.*

*LEFT Symbols reinforce your intentions, and you can imbue precious and treasured objects, such as these jewel-encrusted eggs and ornaments, to make them potent symbols of power. Every time you look at them you will be reminded of the goals or dreams you have associated with them.*

# WATER

Very few people use real water as an interior design feature except in bathrooms and kitchens, and yet it can be a wonderful addition to a home. Water carries important metaphors about the energies of life. Its hidden depths are a source of wisdom, so staring into it provides opportunities for contemplating the deeper meaning of life. Traditionally, people believed that water had sacred power and that it flowed from the very source of spiritual life; over time it has retained a nurturing and healing energy.

Water stimulates and refreshes chi energy. Bring it into your home by buying or creating an indoor fountain or waterfall, with a pump constantly running to re-circulate the water. The sound it makes can be very soothing, but make sure you can adjust it so that it feels comfortable for you. If it sounds too much like a dripping tap you could find yourself wanting to visit the bathroom more frequently.

Introducing a water feature is the ideal way to enhance the energy of your career area. It can also be used outside the house where a corner of the bagua is missing, so if your area of fortunate blessings lies in the backyard, install a small pond there, or at least put in a bird bath. Because of its life-giving qualities, water is strongly associated with money so a water feature or a thirsty plant that needs regular watering placed in any wealth area will boost finances and luck.

Of the five energies, tree energy is boosted by water so the two areas of the bagua associated with it, Elders (3) and Fortunate Blessings (4), would also benefit from water if you wanted to enhance those aspects of your life.

*RIGHT The reason that a fishtank is such a powerful placement in a wealth corner of the bagua of a home or room is not only because it has the element of water, it also has the movement of the fish. As the fish swim in the tank, they increase the stimulation of the energy in that particular place.*

*OPPOSITE Moving water can provide a contemplative setting in which to sit or a powerful enhancement outside a home to a missing wealth area. Of all the places in a home to put a water feature, avoid the areas of Wisdom (8) and the central Health (5).*

*RIGHT A corner of the bagua that needs to be nourished by soil energy (see page 40) can be treated by the introduction of five ceramic pots, in this instance on a mantelpiece. Both the number and the material represent the nature of soil/earth energy.*

*BELOW Positioning a table behind the two armchairs that sit in the middle of a room provides great protection for any occupants who would otherwise be sitting with their backs to the door, feeling vulnerable.*

# PLACEMENT

There are several elements that affect the flow of energy in a room and therefore how we experience it. Where is the room located in the house in relation to the front door? How is the bagua represented in the room and what direction of the compass does it face? What are the predominant colours of the room? What sort of lighting level is there? How many chi enhancers are there, like water, moving objects, windchimes, mirrors, crystals or plants? How is the furniture arranged?

It is the arrangement of furniture that has the biggest impact on how the chi flows around an interior, so how we arrange our space has a direct bearing on how we feel. Following a few simple guidelines will help. Choose only furniture that you love, because anything that has a negative association (because you inherited it from an unpopular relative or the previous owner of the house) drains your energy because you have to look at it or use it all the time. It will help to plan to change pieces whenever you realistically can, so that at least you end up being surrounded only by things you love and enjoy using. Then, keep everything in good repair. Fix anything that is broken. If you are constantly being reminded of the broken chair arm or jammed cupboard door, then this has repercussions throughout your life at some level. If a carpet or chair develops worn areas, cover them with a rug or throw to give them a new lease of life. Then feel the impact of the repair reverberate beyond the room.

When you place things, be mindful of how easy it will be for the chi energy to flow. Every time you make it awkward to enter a room or open a door you should think of this as placing an obstruction somewhere in your life – check which area of the bagua of the house, the room, or the area this is in. If it is awkward making your way through your hall and this part corresponds with your career area, you should not be at all surprised if your attempts to get a promotion are also blocked. Make the room inviting so that it draws in both people and chi. Do not set it up so that it pushes people away or you will end up with an unused room and with at least one aspect of your life that is perhaps a little too quiet.

Chi needs to be able to meander in through the front door, flow gently around your home, nourishing everywhere, and then meander out again. If it were a wind, it would ideally be a gentle breeze, so you need to check that it does not become a hurricane in some places, or get becalmed in others. Sharp angles, corners, ceiling beams and awkwardly placed furniture will all disturb its flow.

Every shape creates a force field around itself so that where there are sharp angles the energy flow is speeded up and projects out from the angle like an arrow or knife. Many Oriental books on feng shui refer to this cutting chi as a poison arrow or killing breath. It becomes extremely uncomfortable to sit under the force of this invisible

*ABOVE  The fabulous curve of this staircase is most impressive and inviting. As it sweeps upwards we cannot see where it will end, which is symbolic of our future: we might know the direction but we do not know for sure how that future will be. Staircases are important for aiding the flow of chi around a home. Here the beautiful curve of the steps and the stairwell encourage that flow. The rectangular panelling acts as a brake to our energy as we descend the stairs, while the placement of the tall display of twigs is a great representation of tree energy, which helps move energy upwards.*

pressure or to be on the receiving end of it as you enter a room. To mitigate its influence, avoid placing a chair next to a corner or square pillar; do not position a refrigerator or large cupboard so that it restricts your energy's movement into the kitchen; place furniture with more strongly defined and less rounded edges diagonally, so the flat side faces a door; screen off hard edges of shelves with drapery; mask corners with plants or choose round edges wherever possible. If you opt for a circular bedside table, for example, it cannot throw a harsh angle at you while you sleep.

Our predominantly geometric architecture means that we have square rooms with corners; and it is here that chi tends to get sucked in and often has difficulty getting out. Once in there it tends to stagnate and this can be made even worse when corners are filled with clutter. Be vigilant about what is stored there, but use a remedy for dark, unfriendly corners too: put in plants or add uplighting which lifts up the chi. When you clean the room, root out the nooks and crannies because it does make a difference. If you ever get the chance to create a space with rounded corners, go for it.

Ceiling beams disturb the flow of chi as it moves across a room, creating a downward pressure at the same time. Too many dark-coloured beams can make a place oppressive and uncomfortable to live in, even if they do look quaint and authentic in your three-hundred-year-old cottage. If they cannot be moved or covered up, make sure that you do not end up sitting or sleeping directly underneath them long term. While a short time might be fine, the pressure is cumulative and you could easily end up feeling unwell or suffering headaches. Lift the chi underneath by bringing in strong, tall plants, uplighting, or symbols of upward movement to rebalance the energies.

ABOVE  When the cook faces away from the kitchen entrance and therefore cannot see directly who is coming in, the placement of this shiny pan on the stove means an eye can be kept on the comings and goings.

LEFT  The circular table and its round pot in the centre are inviting shapes which help to draw in a group of people for a creative discussion. The placement of nine rectangular pictures on the wall next to them will keep conversation structured and practical.

OPPOSITE  Good feng shui is about ensuring a good flow of chi around a home. Light and curved shapes stimulate this flow, while furniture blocking the entrances to rooms or in the walkways will slow it down. Keep doorways clear, and in a living room with many pieces of furniture, it helps to have more natural light and lighter coloured seating to aid the movement of chi.

*RIGHT It is important to have your bed in a good position since you will be spending around one-third of your life in it. The best place is with the protection of a solid wall behind the headboard and with a good view of the door. It should only be moved from this position if you find geopathic stress lines or distortions of natural energy lines in the earth (see page 12) are crossing your bed. The tapestry behind the bed and the cloth-covered circular bedside tables are excellent for softening the environment in which you sleep.*

Where you position your sofa, bed, desk and stove is the most important aspect of furniture placement. The golden rule is to have an arrangement which allows you a good, clear view of the door with some sort of solidity behind you for protection and support. When you sit or stand with your back to the door, you never know when someone is going to come up behind you. When someone surprises a cook working in a kitchen that has a stove facing the door, the cook's energy is momentarily disturbed and this is transferred into the food. Meals prepared in calm, serene environments, on the other hand, are more nourishing. And sleeping with your back to the door can make you nervous as you never really feel settled when asleep.

Finding the right place to sit or sleep in a room is to find the power spot, the place where you feel you have the most control. This will not be in the direct line from the door receiving the strongest flow of chi, because this will be too much. It will be where you have the widest view of the room but are still able to see the main door. Now you can really relax. If you cannot change the position of your sofa, bed or desk, place a mirror so that you can catch an early glimpse of visitors.

*OPPOSITE  We need to have some variety so that our living conditions are not monotonous, always providing the same temperatures, lighting, views and shapes. A conservatory built onto a house can provide two distinct styles, with the brightness in the outdoor room and the darker interior of the house. The change does not, however, want to be too dramatic, otherwise you may end up with extremes of colour and shape which create conflict and jar the nerves. This beautiful room has some shading from both the outdoor trees and indoor shrubs.*

*LEFT  The sofa in this room is the most inviting spot because it has the full protection of a wall behind it and obviously a good view of the door. At the left of the picture is a mirror which is demonstrating a good placement for an area of the bagua that is missing. Mirrors expand energy and will help to compensate where a house is not a complete square and has sections missing.*

# COLOUR

Colour is a manifestation of light and energy; it transforms the world, and through our perceptions of it, can transform our lives. Using colour in our interior decoration allows us to play with, and manipulate, the forces of light and dark and we need both, for our body clocks are attuned to their rhythms, our hormones constantly adjusting to the amount of light available in the day and throughout the year. Thus we rest in the darkness of night and winter, and become more stimulated and active in the daylight and the brightness of spring.

As colour enhances our experience of light and dark we can use it to create a calm, soothing place in which to sleep or a vibrant room in which to talk and play. Colour in our homes is an integral part of our lives because it affects our behaviour, thoughts and feelings. Colour is also associated with emotional properties: being green with envy, sad and blue, red with rage, even having a colourful personality. There is a clear relationship between our energy and that created by colour in an environment. The more we understand how this works, the more we can begin to use it more purposefully to our advantage, creating spaces which help us achieve what we want – a good night's sleep or a bright and optimistic breakfast.

Research has shown that the creation of a mood in a room is more important than arranging it simply for its function. Nowadays rooms are being designed less and less just for eating or watching television. Instead, we are creating places to gather as a family, corners for stimulating conversation, places where we can retreat to wind down and relax, or rooms where we can focus our minds and work on our home computers and browse through our library of books. Colour is a powerful tool in helping us to do this and can have as much effect on the nature of a room as the shape and arrangement of the furniture. It is colour that will determine the overall ambience of a room and will influence how energy behaves in it. And this, in turn, will have a direct effect on our own energy and experience of that space.

## Green

Green is the colour of nature and growth, and because it is at the centre of the colour spectrum it induces feelings of harmony and peace. It soothes the spirit, calms the nerves and reassures people, so it is an appropriate choice as the colour for the international safety code, and to advise traffic that it is safe to proceed. As it is so balancing, green is a very adaptable colour and can be used anywhere – except where you really need to stimulate activity, such as work-related situations. Its restful properties and easy-going nature make it good for bedrooms. But its association with money and abundance mean that you can also use it to stimulate your Fortunate Blessings (4) corner. Add touches of green, perhaps as plants, as a frame around a mirror, or in a tablecloth.

ABOVE  Green is a restful colour but its association with tree energy means that it also represents new growth. Combine this potential with the stripes, which also have an upward, dynamic energy to them, and you create a bright and welcoming place to sit. The orange cushion adds a bold statement to this setting, making it a room more suited to a lively gathering than a quiet retreat.

LEFT  The healing qualities of green make this a very nurturing place with the profusion of plants providing some shade from the sunlight streaming in. The colour blue in the seating also adds to the balanced feeling in the room, making this an ideal place to sit quietly at any time of day and feel both uplifted and refreshed.

*TOP  The green and white flowers represent tree energy which uplifts the fire nature of this wall. It is also balanced by the rectangular earth shapes of the picture and table.*

*ABOVE  A well-balanced environment with the receptive qualities of earth coming from the low shape of the sofa with cushions, and the peach glow on the walls.*

## Red

Red is found sparingly in nature so follow that lead and use it sparingly in your home. It is an extraordinarily powerful colour which grabs attention. It is the first colour that our eyes see so it is used for traffic stop signs and getting noticed. It is not quite what you want in your bedroom, however. It is known to increase your heart rate so a touch of it might inspire passion but too much moves us up the scale towards aggression. You will not feel relaxed if you use it in a dining room either, although the conversation will be stimulating. It is too strong for most interiors but it is ideal for parties and playrooms and it is perfect to use as an accent to catch the eye and stimulate chi flow. It can create a sense of drama and increase fire energy in the area of Illumination (9) if you want to enhance your reputation.

## Purple

Purple is an artistic colour associated with introspection and meditation, clarity, rituals, dignity and a sense of occasion. A dark shade of it would make a very quiet bedroom and it would add grandness to living rooms. Bright purple, however, which has a lot of red in it, is more related to the energy of 'fire' and reputation. Purple is a very regal colour and can be used to create extremely grand and impressive atmospheres. It is also associated with spirituality so a shade of it is ideal for a meditation retreat. Research shows it is also very good for curbing anti-social behaviour.

## Pink

Pink is a calming shade of red and is good for a bedroom because it is very feminine and nurturing. Its healing qualities make it good for children and convalescents and supportive for divorcees. Pink has sedative qualities so it is good for places where you want serenity and for people who have difficulty sleeping. It is a very loving colour that dissipates anger and creates a supportive environment.

## Orange

Orange is a vibrant colour linked to health and vitality. It has developed from the fire of red towards a more earthy tone. Also associated with enthusiasm and optimism, it is a good welcoming colour for hallways, but because it is rather flamboyant, you do have to feel that it suits you or it can be rather overwhelming. Ideal for north-facing rooms which need warming up, it is also a great choice for places where conversation needs to be stimulated.

## Yellow

Yellow represents the sun's power to sustain life and as a stimulating colour it is associated with longevity, cheerfulness and the intellect. To stimulate and focus your mind, sit opposite something yellow when you are writing. This is the colour of earth energy, whose nature is of gathering. This makes yellow a good colour for family rooms and dining areas, but take care not to use it in small spaces as it can make the room feel too intense. It is not a good choice for bedrooms because you want to relax and settle your energy here, rather than making your room feel too gathering and intense.

*ABOVE The red colours of the flowers are impulsive and uplifting. As they will stimulate people and make them feel refreshed, this placement would be good in a morning room or where visitors are received. They would not be appropriate in a reading room or a healing environment as they are too stimulating.*

*OPPOSITE The orange blinds here provide good shade against the excess light and stop too much energy from leaving the room. The colour is extremely lively so this will be a great place for stimulating and intellectual conversation. People will be attracted into the space because of the gathering nature of the yellow and orange. The many other bright colours in the glassware and china make this a vibrant place to eat, although it may prove too much for some people day after day.*

**Brown**

A touch of brown can have a stabilizing effect as it reinforces a connection with the natural world by reminding us of our roots and being grounded. It does have a strong association with autumn and might not be a good choice for older people. It can make a space feel as though it has been used for a long time, for things tend to go brown with age. Depending on the degrees of yellow and red that it contains, brown can be vibrant or murky.

**White**

White represents innocence and purity in our culture. Being devoid of colour it provides a great backdrop, drawing attention to other things like art on the walls. In a stark, monochrome environment with no colour, the focus switches to the people in the place; they then provide the colour and energy. White makes all other things stand out even more. Although useful for some situations, entertaining for example, this might not make for an easy place to live. Bright white is good for bouncing energy around a space like a hallway; off-whites and creams are generally more comfortable to live with.

**Grey**

This is an ambiguous colour and is associated with being in transition or between states. It has the properties of both black and white but is neither one nor the other; it may be viewed as a colour of compromise and harmony, or be seen as dismal and linked to depression. It will be personal choice that determines whether you think it is an ideal neutral background for any room in your house or whether it makes your spirits drop. If you choose this colour for your decor, you will need to keep it fresh-looking.

**Black**

Black absorbs all other colours and creates a sense of depth. If used cleverly, it can create a powerfully stark and impressive atmosphere or an elegant backdrop for other colours; too much used in the wrong way, on the other hand, could make occupants feel very dark and low, even depressed. Black is a mysterious colour which is intriguing and independent. In some cultures it is the colour of mourning and can feel uncomfortable and depressing, while other people will see it as magical and sexy. It can be used to create dramatic backgrounds but is highly inappropriate for children's rooms, dining areas, and places associated with healing.

**Blue**

Representative of the energy of water, blue is associated with introspection, tranquillity and serenity. It is known to reduce inflammation and induce sleep, so it is ideal in the bedroom, particularly with the addition of some warm peach or red accents to reduce its chilling effect. It also reduces tension and stress, so use it in places or situations of conflict, such as offices, or rooms where people have been arguing. It is important to remember that we can have individual reactions to colour. Too much blue for people with little energy will end up making them feel 'blue', so avoid this as a relaxing colour for someone who is prone to low moods.

*ABOVE* The unusual choice of black for the wall transforms this area into an impressive backdrop for a collection of prints. The result is a formal and dramatic presentation for the art, although it would be a very uncomfortable place for relaxation or dining.

*LEFT* The white and pale oatmeal colours in this room make it extremely cool and restful. Any starkness has been moderated by the off-white on the walls and the natural tones in the wood frames of the bed and pictures.

*RIGHT* The blue in this bedroom makes for a potentially cold room but the light wooden floor is warming and its tree energy drains the excess of water created by the colour blue. Orange flowers add a touch of vibrancy to the otherwise restrained decor.

*ABOVE  Here the curves contrast beautifully with the square-tiled floor. The spiral helps take the energy up and down while the floor pattern provides a good foundation to receive you as you move downstairs.*

*ABOVE RIGHT  Round tables provide good focal points in a room and curves, instead of hard square angles, are more relaxing for people sitting around them.*

*RIGHT  The curve at the bottom of these stairs allows the chi to meander more gently back into the hall and makes it more inviting to walk upstairs.*

# SHAPE

Feng shui is the language of symbols and in classical feng shui the masters would interpret the meaning of shapes in the surroundings. Usually they assigned animal archetypes to the contours around a place; they looked for the protection of the land rising behind their houses like the protective shell on the back of a tortoise, and the benevolence of the hill in the east which resembled the shape of a powerful dragon. The idea was to counterbalance the energy emanating from the surroundings by making adjustments to the shape of the interior and in the placement of furniture.

Over time we begin to mirror our surroundings, hence the crooked man in the nursery rhyme lives, where else, but in a crooked house. We are constantly responding to the shapes around us, both consciously and unconsciously. Everything has an effect on us and the most powerful force to shape our lives is the actual shape of the places in which we live. Disjointed and irregular buildings will create disjunctive and unusual lives, whereas, conversely, harmonious surroundings will always help people to feel alive, healthy and balanced.

L-shaped houses are unbalanced because they have something missing and this will be reflected in the inhabitant's life. If the main bedroom is in the wing outside the front door, for example, it is highly likely that family unity will be endangered: one person may even begin to sleep away from home more. Locating the kitchen here will mean that energy for eating is taken out of the home and the occupants will dine out more often. The shape of the house needs to be completed, and this can be done by putting plants and lights outside to add energy to the missing area.

U-shaped houses create a hole in the house, most often in the career area. If you move into a house with this deficiency, you will probably earn more money from betting on losing your job than you will from your employment. A home can be stabilized if you enhance the area outside it with lights, plants and heavy objects like statues or urns to give it as much presence as the interior. Reclaim the space.

Our world is dominated by rectangles and straight lines – the most efficient way to link two places. Long, straight corridors take us from A to B as quickly as possible, with sharp corners creating abrupt changes of direction. The flow of energy is accelerated and our lives, correspondingly, move at a faster pace. In contrast, nature moves more gently, in curves and spirals, and as we move through life, we learn to relish the journey rather than the destination. Curved staircases show us the way forward but there is a mystery at the top because we cannot quite see how things turn out.

Buildings in the shape of a rectangle do not reflect the human body or movement, so our energy does not resonate so well with them; they suit machines and mechanistic thinking. We end up living in square boxes because they are easier and

*ABOVE Shape affects relationships. A round table is ideal for a small group to come together as a community and generate creative ideas and discussions, but circles spin energy away and the meeting is likely to be shorter. Square tables are more suited to discussions about practicalities and for hashing out details. The shape is more sustaining and will hold the energy of the group longer. The roundness of this dining table will bring people together and stimulate a group discussion while its basic rectangular shape lends itself to separate conversations. Notice, also, how the shape of the window arch is echoed in the shape of the table.*

more economic to build on a mass scale, their sharp angles well suited to machine production. The worst scenario arises when we create artificial environments in huge, urban high-rises thinking that they are the only way to survive. However, so far away from nature and landscape and being unable even to see the ground, we cannot connect with natural cycles of change. As we become more and more disconnected from the natural world we begin to feel alienated. Our instincts seek to correct the imbalance by softening harsh environments with curves: an arch at the top of a window, moulded ceiling corners, shelving built into corners, and skirting baseboards smoothing the join between floors and walls. The boxiness of a room can be moderated by a new surround for the fireplace or a recessed area fitted with shelves. Rectangles are good for storage, however, as they help to bring order to chaos by providing discipline and structure. They represent organization and functionality.

Curves and circles hold the energy of creativity and are life-enhancing. They are fluid and organic and stimulate sociability. A balanced and healthy environment blends the two energies and shapes – rectangular and circular. When we understand the function of each shape we can make spaces more effective by putting together the correct blend to support both creativity and functional organization.

Curves and lines have different energies. Circular shapes are dynamic, creative and energetic as they denote movement and are more symbolic of the natural world and the cycles of nature. Rectangles tend to have hard angles and straight lines which accelerate the movement of energy, signify rigidity and firmness, but they also represent organization, practicality and endurance.

LEFT Whether we look at it consciously or not, the way a shape is edged will also have an effect on us. See how this curved triangular table has moulded edges which make it feel much smoother. The squareness of the chairs is also minimized by the unusual light fitting behind and the bowed edges of the sideboard.

FAR LEFT Squares and rectangles represent the human need for order and balance. A combination of squares and circles is a metaphor for an equilibrium between heaven and earth. In this bathroom, the squareness of the mirror and tiled walls is balanced with the round basins, lights, shells and boxes.

BOTTOM LEFT Wherever possible, make an effort to introduce curves and softness into a space, like these doors which help to change a room from an uncomfortable box into something more calming.

RIGHT Part of the charm of an old, traditional home is that the lines are not completely straight. In modern, purpose-built homes, the architecture is regimented and boxy. As we make additions, it helps to break up the lines by adding items like these curved shelves, which are much more harmonious and interesting than a square shelf unit.

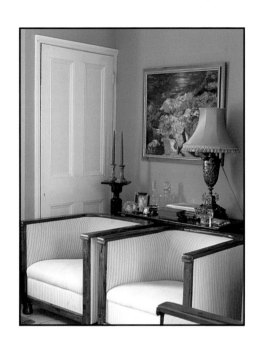

# CASE
# STUDIES

entrances halls & stairs living rooms kitchens bedrooms bathrooms children's rooms work spaces

Our front door gives a strong message to the outside world of who we are. The classical proportions of this entrance make it impressive and grand. The matching pillars, plants and lamps to either side of the doorway create a strong sense of balance, which in turn suggests that the occupants will be reliable and steady; the bright yellow reflects a happy, fun-loving household.

The entrance influences our feelings and thoughts every time we either enter our home or go out into the world: the height of the pillars here will give an uplifting feeling to all those who pass between them. Any irritations you encounter as you enter your home, meanwhile, will simply be replicated in your life: the urn in the doorway here is a little too large. Moving it would make the hallway feel more open and receptive, and would also have a positive bearing on the life of the family living here.

If there are a number of doors leading off the hall, leave open only the one to the main welcoming area – most likely the living room. The room seen from the door usually influences occupants and visitors alike.

# ENTRANCES, HALLS & STAIRS

*Entrances are the connection between the outer world and the inner world of our home, and signify how we relate to society. The more welcoming the entrance, the easier the flow of energy, people, resources and opportunities into our lives.*

Entrances are the gateways of chi energy into the home so they should be free of any obstructions. It is important to make an entrance visible, particularly if it is to the side of the house and hidden from the road. Moreover, it should be clearly demarcated – either with plantings, or with statues and ornamental door guardians – and it should be well lit. The more difficult it is for people to find your door, the more difficult it is for opportunity to knock on it.

The front door is the anchorpoint for the placement of the bagua; it is the source of chi energy for a building, just as our mouths are doorways through which nourishment enters our bodies. If a tree is blocking the doorway or your front path, it can act as a block for people coming into your life. If your entrance is small and narrow, or opens straight into a wall, you need to attract more chi into the house. Make sure the door opens fully as any hindrances will reduce the flow of chi; if you have to push the door because it has warped or catches on the mat, you will find it hard to have a smooth journey in life. If your future direction is unclear, then check that you have good lighting outside and that it is working. And sometimes fixing a broken doorbell is enough to prompt job offers or a more active social life through stimulating helpful friends.

If you have an apartment, your front door is the internal one inside the building but the condition of the shared corridors and main entry point will also have an effect on you. Make sure that the area immediately outside your own entrance is brightly lit and well decorated.

Hallways also create a transitional space and should be as free of distracting objects as you can make them, in order to make the transition from the exterior to the interior world as smooth as possible. Storing things tidily will not only give a better, cleaner first impression, it will also allow a better flow of chi. Similarly, it is good to make a space in the hall to leave outside shoes, as this keeps the energy of the outside world away from the interior world of your sanctuary.

The entrance has now been marked out and made more visible with a pair of small trees and shrubs. A boot scraper outside a front door is something else that helps to define an entrance. Walking past the plants every day will make people feel more positive and uplifted. They will also provide energetic protection against sounds, pollution and traffic in this busy city neighbourhood.

There is a large knocker, which is good, but there is nothing to hold onto to open or close the door. It looks solid and heavy and so does need a good, strong handle. Placing one on the door will help the owner to get a firmer grip on her future direction.

To keep the messy area beyond the door from sight, a screen has been made from garden fencing and used as a shield. It would also be good to grow ivies and colourful plants up this trellis fence.

The owner can also make adjustments inside her hallway to help support her career change. Inspirational images with moving water are good, but she could also add specific symbols associated with healing. A noticeboard with invitations to events and information on her new career would also be helpful, as would a plant on a shelf.

After

**Before**

The owner of this three-storey, semi-detached house has recently moved here from a very cramped two-bedroomed apartment with her husband and two children. She has one nine-year-old son and has just had her second child, so she is currently on maternity leave from her legal job. She does not enjoy the particular aspect of law in which she is working so she is developing a long-term plan to move herself out of this field and into something else, although she is not sure what. She is interested in healing and is considering homeopathy. She loves creative writing and might like to combine that skill in her new career by writing about health. As her main concern is the planning of her new career, the entrance, which sits in the main Journey (1) area of the house, will be the key focus of this consultation.

This four-bedroomed house is on a very busy main road – so having the front door around the side gives the house greater protection. It is important to make an entrance visible, particularly if it is to the side of the house and hidden from the road. Entrances should be well lit and clearly marked out and this can be done with plantings, or with ornamental door guardians and statues. These can be Chinese lion dogs (as traditional feng shui books advise) but equally any animal which you feel signifies protection is fine and these could include lions or dogs. Placing them will increase your sense of security and when you do, have a strong intention for the results you want. This entrance is rather hidden but there are outside lanterns to either side of the door.

The approach to the door from the gate gives a clear view of three refuse bins and the rubbish sacks around them. First impressions are important, so it is not a good idea to have the refuse as the only feature of this courtyard. The nourishing quality of the chi energy which flows into the house has been adversely affected by flowing round the refuse on its way in. The goal is to get as much healthy, vibrant chi into the house as possible. This will also come in the form of light and colour, and the stained glass panel above the door is a delightful way of bringing in colourful, stimulating energy.

Changes to the hallway itself will have a positive influence on the whole house, too, because everybody has to walk through here. They will have the most impact on her career, because the intention was to focus on this aspect of her life, but they will probably have a positive impact on her husband as well. If he wished to make changes in his career, some art with a focus on his future could be featured, or he could simply become involved in choosing the artwork – to make it meaningful for him, too.

The front door lets in a lot of light as it has an inset arched window and panels of coloured stained glass above.

On the window, it is inappropriate to have ornaments of fierce-looking animals, particularly on a glass shelf – these are about as comfortable as a bull in a china shop. They are best removed from the entrance so that they don't symbolically keep people away.

As well as stimulating the missing energy, coloured glass bottles and vases make a bright first impression when people arrive, and their sparkle provides a light, uplifting energy for going up the stairs. The glass of the shelves and bottles, made from sand, represents the energy of earth which stimulates the missing Wisdom (8) energy, helping the search for peace of mind.

Wisdom can be further enhanced by hanging a faceted round crystal in the window at the bottom of the stairs.

The plant on the table at the foot of the stairs has been changed from a poinsettia to a blue hyacinth as this colour, synonymous with water, stimulates the house of the Journey (1). Blue plants have also replaced the dried flowers in the window.

Before

The owner of this semi-detached house is married with three children under twelve. A family house, the property is essentially square with the exception of a section missing in the area of Wisdom (8), which falls to the left of the front door – in the garage. This area cannot be counted in the bagua because it is not lived in.

The owner is currently a full-time mother but she would like to go back to work part-time. She is not sure what she would like to do and is considering retraining in another field. She feels very creative but does not get much chance to express herself, although she does enjoy making curtains and painting furniture for her home. She is not sleeping well and so she feels tired constantly, and therefore cannot make the most of her days. Her priority is to support her family emotionally but this sometimes means she has less time for herself. She would like to have some quiet time, and both she and her husband feel that this is missing from their lives. The main issues to address now, therefore, are the houses of the Journey (1), Wisdom and Creativity (7).

What people see when they first enter a house – whether they are inhabitants or visitors – will influence their experience. Having a flat wall facing you is the best solution, rather than a partial view of a wall, and then an open area or corridor. Flowers on a shelf or half-moon side table are welcoming. The hallway here is wide and there is a good open corridor with a sideboard and display at the end. At the moment, however, it tends to collect clutter. The stairwell to the left of the hall has a banister with a beautiful curve at the bottom but this tends to be obscured by coats. With three children in the household, there is obviously a lot of coming and going through the front door; clutter quickly accumulates.

The entrance is sitting in the Journey, the career area of her house, so it is a good room to be the focus of this consultation as everything here will have a bearing on her future. Conversely, anything blocking this part of the house will have an adverse effect on the occupant's search for a new career.

**After**

The first sight when the door is opened is the large sideboard at the end of the hall opposite the front door, which is a perfect collecting point for mail, keys, shopping and anything waiting to go upstairs. Regular clearing of these clutter points is essential: not only is it unsightly – particularly as the sideboard is the first thing you see when you enter the house – but it would cause stagnation of energy.

The character of the arrangement on and above the sideboard has been changed from tall and spindly to more solid: square picture frames are displayed with a cluster of potted plants, giving a greater sense of stability.

There was a chair halfway along the hall, which tended to collect coats and scarves and no one ever sat on it. It was creating an unnecessary blockage. It has been removed because the aim is to allow as much free-flowing energy as possible to circulate through her home and life.

The wall to the right of the door was empty and as it is sitting in the Creativity (7) part of the hall, it is an ideal place to put an image which would support the career search. As she is not sure what she wants to do and cannot choose a specific image symbolic of her new career, art depicting flowing water or any decorative map will help her find her way forward.

A bright red welcoming rug produces a surge of energy when you look at it. It has been placed on the floor to further stimulate the occupant's career.

The area of Wisdom (8) is missing from the house and is affecting the occupant's peace of mind and her ability to know what is the right career move. It needs energizing and a mirror has been placed on the wall at

After

**Before**

the bottom of the stairs, having been moved
from above the sideboard. This will open up
the space and make it feel that the part of
the house that is missing is actually there.

At the same time, the convex mirror
replacing the oval one at the end of the hall
creates flexibility and direction, and enables
people to see around the corner.

## TIPS FOR ENTRANCES & HALLS

• Mark out your territory and make your entrance clearly distinguishable from the rest of the doorways on your street – with lights, hanging baskets, trees and a clearly presented name and number.

• If you do have a house number, ensure that the digits are placed in an upward swing from left to right as the focus of our future is in the right of a frame.

• Set the mood for how you and your visitors experience the house, using mirrors and positive artworks with lots of perspective.

• Keep halls and corridors clear of clutter and obstructions; they will have a negative impact on you every time you come home. Keep up-to-date with your mail: neatly store away anything dealt with.

• Don't overwhelm and confuse visitors with busy artworks and decor. Carpets are better plain or with a small pattern.

• If halls and corridors are very long, the chi must be slowed down. Break up a view from the front to back of your home with a windchime; small, rounded plant containers on the floor; or paint motifs on the wall to distract the eye – a stencil of a vine or ivy has movement and will have the same effect.

• Do not offer the chi in the home easy ways to escape: stairs that are rounded at the bottom will turn the energy back inside. Or reflect it with a mirror or shiny object behind the front door or at the top of the stairs.

**LEFT** The hall is where you set the mood for how you and your visitors will experience the rest of the house. This rich flower arrangement gives a positive welcome and reflects the host's hospitality. The bright yellow of the walls is good for gathering energy and the round-cornered table keeps it smooth-flowing. The pictures up the stairwell help to move the energy upwards.

**ABOVE** Keep hallways and corridors clear of obstructions so that you can achieve the maximum flow of energy. The beautiful curved wall here provides a smooth passageway for the energy. The area is made more welcoming by the plant that has been put onto a small round table.

**LEFT** Marking the presence of your doorway clearly is always beneficial, and this is beautifully achieved here with the matching pairs of urns, trees and boot irons. Symmetry always adds a sense of rhythm and balance. Where there is a long vista from the door or window, your attention tends to get lost on the horizon and your energy diffused. Here the statue in the garden brings attention back to the foreground and helps the occupants of the house to feel more focused and grounded.

**LEFT** Shiny door fittings encourage more chi into the home and also protect you from the negative influence that occurs if a road comes straight towards your house.

# LIVING ROOMS

*Today's living rooms are both the most public part of the home and the hub of family life, the place where we live together and entertain visitors. They need to be comfortable, well-lit spaces where we proudly display our favourite possessions.*

Whereas in the past living rooms had different names and functions – drawing room, morning room, parlour and sitting room – today's living rooms are multi-functional. They are the main gathering places where we receive visitors, but are also the part of the home where we relax, watch television, talk or read. The space should be arranged to suit both uses, being welcoming – rather than too formal – and comfortable. This is the most public part of the home and should be nearer the front entrance than the kitchen (and the bedrooms in the case of an apartment or bungalow). It is important that the arrangement of furniture and the colour scheme make the room inviting.

When arranging seating, try to place chairs and sofas at slight angles, rather like the sides of the octagon of the bagua; chairs sitting directly opposite each other create a more formal environment. It is best not to have any seats with their backs to the door, and important to make sure that the host's chair is in the command position, facing the door and with the protection of a wall behind it. Visitors, who are not there all the time, can sit with the more open aspect behind them. Clusters of chairs arranged to face a television will let the television dominate the room, making communication difficult. Arranging chairs around a hearth is infinitely preferable. A fireplace usually creates the ideal focal point in a room and, with its warmth, is a welcoming sight. If it is too hot, and hard to relax, the intensity can be reduced by cooling with a mirror above it and plants to either side. For creating balance, place pairs of objects on the mantelpiece.

The living room is where you should display your art collections and precious antiques. Make sure you choose well, that you really like the pieces and that they are true reflections of you, because whatever you choose gives clues about your personality and aspirations to visitors. You will also have to look at them every day.

Arrange furniture so there is an easy flow of energy and avoid too many tables and clutter. It is in this room that energy will collect and then disperse around the house and family. Keep that energy bright and clear, and allow it to move freely. Windows with views are good, but take care not to have walls of windows as too much energy will be lost through the wide open space and the room will feel less nurturing.

Where you have big, splendid views from your windows, add plants to the windowsill to bring your focus back into the room, otherwise your valuable energy will be dispersed unnecessarily. Plants by windows also act as powerful protection against negative influences from the outside: nearby trees, lamp posts and busy roads, for instance. Here, the climbing tree on the patio just outside the door keeps the focus in the foreground but at the same time does not inhibit views of the garden.

Being able to alter the amount of bright light in a room is helpful, because the energy requirements of a living room vary according to its different roles. Blinds and soft drapes with a scooped fringe top provide flexibility with the right amount of light and soften the otherwise hard lines.

Electrical items tend to draw our attention and energy rather insistently. Make a clear distinction between the focal point of the room and the television. Indeed, try to hide the television inside furniture or with a screen. Don't let it dominate the surroundings. If you don't have a fireplace, arrange the seating around a central table like this, with a large display of flowers.

The occupants of this large, semi-detached, early Victorian house have lived here for seven years. During this time, the couple have done extensive renovation work throughout the building. Our consultation reveals four areas of their lives that are priorities to consider. The wife feels stress in relation to her career and is busy trying to move from the job that earns her a living to that of garden design, which she feels very strongly is her true vocation. This indicates problems with the Journey (1) area of the bagua, as well as the area of Creativity (7), because she has trouble finding the time to devote to the work that gives her the greatest feeling of creative satisfaction.

We also need to look carefully at the area of Wisdom (8). With so much stress involved in her career transition, she finds it difficult to set aside time for quiet reflection. Her husband, who has recently set up his own business and runs an office from home, is enjoying his work but also finds little time for contemplation. Moreover, he does not feel particularly blessed, and the couple have some problems with finances, suggesting that the Fortunate Blessings (4) area of their lives is blocked. More positively, both are in good health and feel that they have many close friends on whom they can rely. This indicates that the Health (5) and Helpful Friends (6) areas of their lives are working very well, so there is no need to make adjustments to these areas of the house.

More than any other room, the living room gives strong signals to the world about our personality, hopes and dreams: it is probably our most public room. The art the couple has selected for the walls, the mementoes collected from their trips around the world, the books they read, their choice of magazines and ornaments – all these things define who they are. If they start to change these, they will begin their redefinition of themselves.

The crowded nature of this living room, where there is really far too much furniture, reflects the crowded nature of their current lives. There is not enough time for them to do the things they really enjoy, and as a consequence they feel very stressed. The pressure on them will be relieved as soon as they take pressure off the space, and opportunities will open up when they remove the physical obstacles in the room that are blocking them.

**After**

**Before**

A redundant doorway in the career area of the living room was blocked off by a chair, indicating a blockage in the corresponding area of the occupants' lives. A tapestry has been hung over the unused entrance to disguise the door, removing the sense of confusion that might prevail here. The chairs that were blocking the space, making the movement of chi and of people difficult, have been taken away. Although the owners were very fond of them, the chairs were simply too large for the space. The table has been cleared of magazines and many of the ornaments to reduce the sense of clutter.

This living room was previously two smaller rooms, and consequently it is split in half by a beam; this has been the focus of much attention as it affects the seating. The sofa was too close to the beam, so people who sat there were adversely affected by a downward pressure of energy; the area between the chest and the light fittings was too small for the large picture hanging there. Both the picture of the hot-air balloon and the existing light, which points upwards under the beam, were good corrections for the downward pressure in this area, but the painting was far too large.

The unused fireplace was filled with twigs, pine cones and dried leaves. Alongside was an iron coal bucket filled with logs. The display seemed tired, dusty and out of season. There were no plants or fresh flowers in the room, only bowls of pot pourri, reinforcing a lack of movement and an overwhelming feeling of stagnation.

There were also three broken clocks, all displaying frozen moments of time, one in the area of Fortunate Blessings (4).

As well as being overcrowded, the room felt very awkward and needed to be made calmer, which also helps to address the fact that the area of Wisdom (8) is missing both from the living room and from the floorplan of the house. This undermines the occupants' ability to deal with stress.

The chairs on either side of the sideboard have been removed, to improve the feeling of spaciousness. The large painting has been replaced by a smaller image so that the whole area is no longer crowded. The pile of magazines on the shelf below is now considerably smaller – only a precious few have been retained. The pile can now be

Before

viewed as neat storage instead of clutter, but it will still need regular sorting out.

The pair of colourful ethnic dolls sitting on the mantelpiece in the Relationships (2) area has been retained. However, the pair of pictures has been replaced with a single, uplifting image: the large picture of the hot-air balloon previously hung above the sideboard. This should help the owner to focus single-mindedly on her new career.

Last year's 'forest fruit' harvest and pot pourri have been replaced by several vibrant plants to symbolize new growth. With garden design as the proposed new career, bringing the natural world indoors is especially helpful; to have more nature around will make it easier for the owner to realize her future in the present.

**After** *above and left*

**Before**

The owner of this apartment and her fiancé like living here but both feel stressed. The apartment has one master bedroom (see pages 118–19) and a second bedroom that is triangular in shape and only big enough to use for storage. The remaining rooms are a tiny kitchen and bathroom and the main living area shown here. The couple finds the apartment very small and they miss having space to themselves. Where people lack quiet space in their lives, in terms of time or an actual place, the area of Wisdom (8) needs to be addressed.

Both occupants work very long hours. Although they enjoy their work, they would like to use their creativity. Their personal relationship is good but they have concerns about money, despite their high salaries.

The room is quite busy with a lot of heavy furniture. It is also on a direct route from the front door to the rest of the house, making it hard to relax and settle. The large, wooden-framed mirror in the centre of the room provides a strong focal point and expands the space, but there is a television beneath it which has become too strong a focus. As both occupants expressed a need for quiet and more time to relax, it would be better to diminish the influence of the television.

There are big contrasts in this room with too many strong images and textures making a small space even smaller. The mirror and tall cabinet are overpowering and the space feels more crowded by the dark mustard-yellow walls. Ideally, these should be painted lighter to reduce the intensity in the room and the contrast. The key areas to work on are the Journey (1), Fortunate Blessings (4), Creativity (7) and Wisdom.

**Too many dried flowers and bunches of dried roses were stagnating the chi energy in this room. One bunch was displayed in the Journey (1) area and there was another in Wisdom (8). These have been thrown out, as have the two plants in the Wisdom area, which were obstructing a narrow passageway. This relieves the stress in this particular area.**

**The three large shelves in the Journey were too cluttered and full of books. There was discord and tension, and the situation was compounded by the clutter being reflected in the large mirror above the fireplace. The area has been opened up by taking everything off the top shelf and adding two paintings. By choosing fashion as the theme for the pictures, the owner has introduced tangible symbols of her future into the present, which makes it appear both more real and achievable.**

The Fortunate Blessings (4) area in the room was blocked by a large, tall, wooden cabinet set at an angle in the corner. This has been straightened and uplighting placed next to it. The dried flowers and spiky yucca plant next to the cabinet which made the chair feel uncomfortable have been replaced with a round-leaved bushy plant placed behind the chair.

The windows of the living room are dirty, obscuring the view to the outside world and making it harder to have clarity and envision new possibilities. Cleaning will bring some brighter energy into the home.

To reduce the attraction of the television as the focal point in the room, a firescreen featuring an attractive red tapestry with a flame-like pattern has been placed in front of it. The shelves below the television have been cleared and excess books removed.

There was a brown leather sofa sitting in the Elders (3) area which was old and had broken springs, so it offered no support. The energy was sagging and this was reflected in a lack of energy opposite the bagua in Creativity (7). As the owner needs as much support and encouragement as possible for her creativity, the advice for the sofa is to remove, replace or repair it.

A beam divides the centre of the room but it is painted white, the colour of the ceiling, and it has lights mounted into it which reduce its impact. The occupants should avoid sitting directly underneath it.

The low table in the centre was practical but made it awkward to walk around the space, especially as this is the main route through the apartment from the front door. It has been replaced with a smaller fabric-covered one with softer corners.

**After** *left*     **Before** *above*

There was a great deal of tree energy in the room, represented by the tall wooden cabinet and the large wooden mirror. This added too much upward, dynamic energy into the room so it needed to be soothed. The occupants have chosen an oval tablecloth in an off-white to reduce the tree presence in the room (white and circular shapes represent metal energy which controls tree). In the future, a circular rug in cream could be placed on the wooden floor.

ABOVE  When it is lit in the colder months, a fireplace looks very welcoming, but for much of the year it can seem a rather dark area in a room. Displays of seasonal plants are ideal for lifting the energy here.

RIGHT  This corner table, with its flowers and hidden light, combined with a mirror, is a great way of brightening a dark corner and for enhancing a specific area of the bagua, particularly that of Fortunate Blessings (4).

OPPOSITE  People feel most at ease and comfortable when they are in control of their surroundings. Ideally, seating should be supported by having a solid wall behind it. If this is not possible, there should at least be a clear view of the door.

### TIPS FOR LIVING ROOMS

• Round tables are much more comfortable to gather around in informal settings than square or rectangular ones.

• Avoid glass-topped tables, especially those that don't have frames, as it is not possible to relax fully around the sharp edge of glass.

• Yellow is a great colour for gathering energy and people, and is generally a good choice for living rooms. You will not be able to relax if the yellow is too intense, and avoid using it in small spaces.

• Fresh-cut flowers keep energy refreshed – a worthwhile investment. Dried flowers hold stagnation; change them seasonally.

• Ensure that you leave enough floor space to allow for people congregating. Do not overfill the room with furniture.

• If you have ceiling beams, do not place a seat directly underneath them. Anyone sitting there regularly may begin to suffer from headaches.

• Position chairs so that they do not face a corner or anything sharp; the cutting chi will be unsettling and disturbing.

• Displays of pictures of your family – photographs or paintings – will reinforce a sense of cohesion in the household.

• Create a clear focal point in the room which is not the television or it will dominate the surroundings.

Although the country cottage look may not be to everyone's taste, it is good to avoid the glaring brightness of fast-food kitchens – shiny fittings and a lot of harsh metal – in your home. They may look clean and bright but they have a more stressful influence on the food. Whatever you can introduce in the way of natural objects and materials will make your space more cosy and relaxing, and will positively affect both food preparation and eating. Or counter the hardness of metal and marble in a more austere space by balancing it out with natural, rustic and woven materials.

Lighter colours make both a kitchen and dining room more soothing. Greens and yellows are good for kitchens, but tones in the red spectrum can be effectively used for occasional dining if you are looking for stimulating conversation.

It is always best to work in the brightest and most open spaces. So good lighting is very important in kitchens; all corners and preparation areas must be fully illuminated. Candlelight, or at any rate focused lighting, is better for dining areas.

# KITCHENS & DINING ROOMS

*The roles of both the kitchen and the dining room are essential in creating and maintaining our good health, because the food we cook and eat generates new life within us.*

The kitchen is the heart of the home. It is also the most important room as regards our nourishment – both physical and spiritual – so it is vital that the person who actually carries out the cooking in the house does so in an atmosphere of calmness and with the minimum disturbance. Any jarring interruptions will affect the cook's energy. Similarly, our own energy levels are dependent on our ability to absorb nutrients from food, and this is severely diminished if the kitchen environment is chaotic and untidy. It must be clean, orderly and free from clutter, and there should be plenty of space, good organization and storage to encourage a steady flow of chi. Make sure that food preparation areas are not situated in corners which are exposed to the negative force from a sharp angle or shelf.

Where the kitchen is situated in the home has a bearing on family life. If the kitchen appears to be 'outside' the building, protruding from the front door as an extension, then the occupants are likely to eat out often. If it is clearly visible from the front door, then food will be your focus whenever you arrive home. And if your visitors come into your house through the kitchen, or can see it easily, they will more than likely end up sitting around the dining table. A key factor to harmony in the kitchen is the location of the stove in relation to the door, sink and window (see page 108).

It is best to eat in a comfortable place in an unhurried atmosphere. Avoid being distracted by stimulating pictures on the walls, or clutter and mess on the table. The principal elements in a kitchen are water and fire. Tree energy balances these two elements, so it is good to use wood and the colour green in the kitchen. Ideally, the dining table will be in a separate room, but if it is in the kitchen, make sure that before you eat you clear away cooking utensils and draw attention away from the kitchen functions, either by dimming the lighting, or by screening it off. Put a good light above the dining table or use candles, rather than having a bright general light in the room.

**Before**

The couple who own this large, four-bedroom house have lived here for just three months; they loved it the first time they saw it. Apparently they shared a taste with the previous occupants for simple, natural environments – large areas of empty space, fresh white walls and a natural jute floor covering throughout. However, the previous occupants had three children and the house is both designed for, and well used to, supporting a family, and the predecessor energy in the house is strongly oriented towards family life. The owners, meanwhile, have known each other for over twenty years and do not want children. So they need to change the energy and claim the space for themselves and their work. There is no reason why the house cannot support business projects, providing that the intention is clearly placed into the space.

The galley kitchen lies between the hall and the dining room in the centre of the house. The decor is very bare and the combination of grey marble and white tiles is harsh and stark. In fact, the whiteness in the house generally is very intense and needs to be softened. Likewise, the dining room feels very austere, making it very hard to feel nurtured there. The couple need to create a more nourishing environment for the areas where they make and eat their food, or else food will begin to lose its sustenance.

The dining room is an extension which has been built on to the house, creating a missing area in Fortunate Blessings (4) at the back of the house. The woman, who is in her late thirties, needs a creative outlet away from her work and a garden would provide this, ensuring that she spends time with the earth, which would help her relax.

The kitchen and dining room are to be examined and adjusted because they are having the most impact on the occupants' health and their experience of their home: she is suffering from one cold after another, he has tinnitus and so needs to protect himself, and neither of them are really being nourished.

**As health issues specifically needed attention, the focus of the consultation was on creating a nurturing environment. The kitchen felt very stark because there was an abundance of shiny metal – from pans, kettle and fruit bowl, to bottle rack and salt and pepper shakers, all made of chrome or stainless steel. The introduction of natural materials in this kitchen has softened the intensity and harshness.**

**A large wooden chopping board and wooden plate rack, symbolic of tree energy,**

have been placed on the counter between the sink with its water energy and the stove's fire energy to harmonize the energy flowing constantly between the two.

Modern, high-tech kitchens may look stunning but they can be uncomfortable rooms in which to spend any length of time. The combination of natural wood with the greenish blue of the painted doors is an excellent colour choice for a kitchen, but the room still appeared and felt very bare and stark. So, baskets of vegetables and pots of fresh growing herbs have been brought in to increase the feeling of naturalness and to soften the overall effect. The addition of more wood makes the kitchen feel more homely and less sterile and this will be reflected in the nourishing quality of the food cooked here.

While money is not a problem at the moment, Fortunate Blessings (4) lies in a negative space. To address this, and the considerable – and potentially health-threatening – stress that settling bills still causes the woman who lives here, a piece of mirror glass the same size as the cooking rings can be fixed to the wall behind the stove; this would symbolically double the wealth of the household.

**After** *above and below*

The dining room was empty except for a round dining table and four director's chairs, making it a great space for entertaining but much less comfortable for day-to-day living – and certainly not cosy for two.

Although the occupants are not having problems with their relationship, it is always good to protect areas of your life which *are* working, especially in any new situation, or new home. As it is, the couple is aware that their many individual commitments in the evenings mean that they lack quality time together. Making the experience of eating together cosier would help. And being situated in the Relationships (2) area of the house, the room is ideally placed to focus on strengthening their life together.

To remove any sense of time pressure from meals the wall clock has been removed and replaced by a landscape characterized by earth tones of peach and yellow, which will strengthen relationships, and warm shades of pink, associated with romance and nurturing. In time, it would be a good idea for the couple actually to commission a painting or photograph with an emphasis on yellow (the colour of soil energy): a pair of bright sunflowers would be good.

More generally, the room needed to be given a gathering nature, and though the round table is good, it was very bare. Round orange fruits in a round dish on the round table have great gathering energy, providing a good focal point to draw people in. The simple cotton cloth, meanwhile, both softens the look and reinforces feelings of warmth and nurture. Although it does not fall in the area of Helpful Friends (6), this room has now become a place where friends will feel welcome.

Before

The atmosphere of the room can be altered according to the season, by moving in new plants and changing the colour of the tablecloth: fresh greens would be good for spring, cool blues for summer and yellows for autumn. This sun room, with two walls and a ceiling made from glass, is quite exposed so needs more symbols of gathering energy, especially in winter. Terracotta, ceramics and plants, plus warmer red tones and earth colours, will all make the room more comfortable.

The ceiling is high but art on the walls and plants around the table will bring the eye down. The plain wall on the left is in Elders (3), ideal for pictures of the couple's families. Generally, pictures that feature both themselves and their parents will help to heal past difficulties and promote harmony.

A small crystal hung in the window onto the patio would help to support the missing Fortunate Blessings (4) area. To protect what wealth there is, the patio must be well lit and have pots with bright plants.

**LEFT** Try to avoid placing the table in a busy crossroads area, or having too many doors opening onto it, because this will make the food much more difficult to digest. Nor should the table sit directly in the line of unsettling cutting chi, which will project from all sharp corners. The flowing lines of this set of wall shelving, on the other hand, actively enhance the relaxed feel that has been created in this setting.

**RIGHT** The location of the stove can have a big impact on the quality of your food. The cook should not face directly away from the door, nor should the stove be below a window, because vital energy is lost through the glass and external wall. Ideally, a triangular arrangement is created with the stove, sink and refrigerator, and as fire is the most natural cooking medium, gas is the first choice for cooking rather than electricity. Wooden dining tables provide good, solid support and are preferable to uncomfortable glass ones.

**LEFT** Wherever possible, try to introduce smooth lines and curves into a space rather than sharp angles; this will encourage the energy to flow more evenly around the room. This circular table and rounded kitchen cabinet help to make this kitchen-dining area a more nourishing place.

**RIGHT** Avoid displaying abstract art in a dining area or your unconscious mind will be trying to work out what is going on in the image while you are eating. One of these quirky pictures depicts a road junction with the appropriate message 'Slow'.

**TIPS FOR KITCHENS & DINING ROOMS**

• The stove, sink and refrigerator should form a triangle. Where a sink is next to a stove, put a wooden chopping board between them to maintain the balance between tree, fire and water energies.

• A shiny, metal toaster or kettle in front of a cook with his or her back to the door – and a windchime near the doorway – alerts the cook to anyone coming into the kitchen.

• The refrigerator can face the door as you will spend the least time standing in front of it. Ensure it is full of fresh food, as this symbolizes prosperity in the household.

• Good lighting is essential: the cook must be able to see all food preparation areas.

• Good ventilation is important: the heat and vapours generated by cooking should not permeate the rest of the house.

• No clocks: create a timeless and unhurried environment in which to eat.

• When creating a kitchen from scratch try to customize units and surfaces to fit the person who will be doing the cooking.

• Think of bright, shiny fast-food restaurants and try to create the antithesis: use natural materials whenever possible.

• Lighter colours make a dining room more soothing, but tones in the red spectrum can be used for occasional dining to stimulate conversation.

# BEDROOMS

*A bedroom needs to be a nurturing retreat which will soothe you at the end of a long and active day, far away from the noise and stress of the outside world. It should be a sanctuary where deep relaxation and rejuvenation are inevitable.*

Increasingly, people are beginning to recognize that having too much to do and being subjected to an overload of information causes constant and incredible stress. This means that what you need at the end of the day is a nurturing retreat, not a place of stimulation and distraction, nor somewhere to entertain. One of the greatest gifts you can give yourself is to create your bedroom as a sanctuary with as few things as possible to stimulate the eye or the mind.

Ideally, you should sleep in a small room where the energy is more settling and contained, having removed everything from the room that might affect the quality of your sleep. All the clothes you have worn during the day which have picked up energies from the world outside should be banished to a separate dressing room or storage area. And although it is often difficult to find the space to do this, rethinking the arrangement of your rooms to facilitate this separation of day and night would make a real difference.

The location and arrangement of your bedroom can make a huge impact on your health and whether you have enough vitality to wake up each morning wanting to jump out of bed. The master bedroom is best located at the back of the house, away from the coming-and-going energy of the front door. When you move into a new house, try sleeping in all the bedrooms and 'feel' the quality of the energy in each before you commit to one. It is best to avoid choosing a room that lies outside the main section of the home. This arrangement can mean that one or both partners will spend a lot of time away from home, which does not bode well for a good relationship. If you live in an apartment in a building, meanwhile, try to avoid sleeping above a busy, public hallway because the constant flow of energy will be unsettling.

Your choice of room should be determined by comfort rather than by size – ideally it should be symmetrical. Corners and nooks work better in living spaces; they make a room busy, whereas a bedroom really needs to be a place of refuge. Look at the room and ensure that there is nothing to disturb you while you sleep – mirrors, electrical appliances, the wrong pictures and vibrant colours – denying you total relaxation and rejuvenation.

Even when you have a big bedroom, you should try to avoid the temptation to fill it with furniture. The occupants of this spacious city apartment have designed a bedroom that inspires tranquillity. In this uncluttered space, they have imported a bigger bed to fill what might otherwise have felt like an overwhelming gap.

The large windows give wide views over the city, and although there is a window behind the head of the bed, its negative effect has been successfully corrected: there are screens to pull across at night to create a 'solid' wall and enclose the space.

The room is characterized by good symmetry and pairing: matching bedside tables and two pictures of couples act as good reinforcements for a relationship. Although not a retreat bedroom, it probably supports its city dwellers quite well, but they should get away to the country at the weekends to help bring a better sense of balance to their lives.

The sunlight paints the room a vivid yellow. This, the strong gathering colour of earth energy, needs to be drained a little and the white bedcover, representing metal energy, effectively settles the stimulus.

**After**

Both occupants like their bedroom stark, white and simple; although the room needed to be made more nurturing and warmed up with brighter colours, any adjustments had to fit in with this style. Cushions and a throw in warm, earth tones have been placed on the bed, creating strong boundaries of colour – for stability in a white room.

The bed's occupants have been suffering because the bed stands directly beneath the downward pressure of a sloping ceiling. The energy needed to be pushed upwards, so a pair of plants has been positioned to either side of the bed, along with two bedside lights – adjustable freestanding uplighters to avoid the clutter of bedside tables and allow for reading, and to light the wall behind too.

There is a door to the storage space behind the bed, which sits off-centre behind one of the sleeping pair. This needed to be covered. Installing a tall wooden headboard fulfills this function and supplies a quantity of tree energy that serves to lift the ceiling behind the bed. If muslin were draped from the headboard up the ceiling, it would further reduce the impact of the downward pressure of the slope and improve the situation. Facing the bed is a sharp corner: the angle of the wall that houses the stairs. A tall plant deflects its cutting chi.

The corner that houses the television has been transformed into a sanctuary for quiet relaxation. As this is the wealth area of the room, plants here would also stimulate good financial activity. A comfy chair makes a safe and tempting refuge from the rest of the house, encouraging more relaxation, prompting the female occupant to be less stressed and thus to give off fewer 'too-busy' signals to her parents.

**Before**

This bedroom is in a large family house situated in an area popular with families, because of nearby schools, but the couple who live here do not plan to have children. They both work freelance, so it is ideal for them to have extra space at home to develop their careers. And indeed, as soon as they moved into this larger house, having found that their last home made them feel claustrophobic, their business opportunities seemed to increase and the woman suddenly found that she had more clients.

She feels split between her work areas. Having been in this state of transition for two years, she feels very pressured; she is struggling financially to maintain her share of the running costs of their home, which she finds extremely stressful; and she has just signed up for a degree course – one more call on her time. He is a researcher and writer, and really enjoys what he does. Their relationship is good, but they find they never have sufficient quality time together. In addition, she feels that they do not have enough time for their friends and feels much less in contact with her social network than she did ten years ago. Generally her relationship with her parents is good, although they feel that she is too busy to spend much time with them. He does not get on so well with his parents but accepts the situation.

Some changes have already been made in the kitchen and dining room, but the converted attic bedroom obviously needs attention as neither party is sleeping well: he has had trouble sleeping since they moved here; she has felt tired for the past year and has already had two colds since moving in. She is always on the go, with no time to be creative and no time for quietness and reflection. The issues for this consultation that we deal with here are sleep quality, Wisdom (8), strengthening the woman's ability to cope with her life now, and Elders (3) to help their family relationships. Helpful Friends (6) to build up their social network and Creativity (7) have been adjusted downstairs.

Feng shui is not just concerned with the energy of places but with the energy of people too. People possess a vibration and this can linger in things in the environment; it is sometimes possible to sense the unhappiness of the previous owners of a space, you can just feel it in the 'vibes'. It is very important to get rid of items that are filled with the previous owners' energy. If it is something that you absolutely adore and would like to inherit, you must make sure you clean it thoroughly. In this room, the previous owner's pink curtain has finally been removed, but this has created another problem: the bed now needs a headboard.

Symmetry, which provides balance, has been created by installing bedside tables. A second round table has been introduced and both have been covered with pale pink cloths; the glass has been removed because this is too hard a material to have next to a bed. Matching plants have been added, too, while the books have been removed.

Electricity still flows through the wiring of appliances even when they are switched off, so it is good to get into the habit of unplugging everything in your bedroom before you go to sleep. Obviously this would be impractical if you had an electric alarm clock. However, because your head, which is the part of the body most susceptible to electro-magnetic radiation, will most likely be lying in the electro-magnetic field of the clock right through the night, it is best to replace the clock with one that runs on batteries, as here.

After

**Before**

The occupants of this three-storey house have lived here for the last two and a half years, and although they are happy, they have not really felt very settled. The children's health has not been good; the mother has been looking to change her career, and she has been ill herself. She feels generally tired and so does her husband; neither of them wake up in the morning feeling really refreshed. And while they generally have a great relationship, they do not feel as close as they might at the moment.

Adjustments that have been implemented in the hall of the house (see pages 84–87) should help progression towards a career change. However, having looked at all the rooms in the house, it seems that it is the master bedroom which is causing problems as regards the couple's health and sleep – or lack of it.

The room is rather cluttered. There is a king-size bed with a busily patterned patchwork cover and large cushions. The bedside tables do not match: one is round with a glass top, the other a small, square side table with many books sitting on the lower shelf. There is a pink curtain behind their bed which was left by the previous owners; the current owners have never liked it but have not got around to taking it away. Meanwhile, the wall at the other end of the bed, which is the first thing that the couple see every morning, is currently blank.

From one side of the bed, there is a view down to the bathroom through a corridor which is used as a dressing area. The husband used to sleep on this side of the bed but recently asked to change sides – for no reason other than he started to recognize discomfort. Now she cannot sleep so well. One of the main problems for the husband is that he has an electric radio/alarm clock on the table next to his head.

**Before**

A simple muslin curtain has been hung to hide the corridor that used to serve as a dressing area; this effectively closes off this secondary space and makes the bedroom itself more regular in shape. The couple now share the same view at the end of their bed, which will also help to harmonize their relationship.

The end of the bed lies in the career area of the room, so it is a particularly important part of the room for her. This space needed to be filled with something inspiring to look at – every morning on waking and every evening before going to sleep. Images of either gently moving water or something related to the area in which she wants to retrain would be equally good in this situation. In the end, she chose a painting of a pretty river with sailing boats.

It is good to set boundaries for your energy while you are in bed – with a headboard and a footboard (or piece of heavy furniture). Although there is still no headboard, this room is large enough to allow a table to be placed at the end of the bed, making a good anchor. The lovely blue china bowl and jug also provide support for career change as the colour blue is associated with water, the house of the bagua representing life's journey, and containers encourage new opportunities.

To make the sleeping environment even more settled, the patchwork bedspread has been replaced by something simpler, with a pattern of gentle waving lines.

The one mirror in the room has been hung at the right height so that both of the occupants can see themselves in full, rather than cutting off the tops of their heads with an adverse effect on their well-being.

**After**

Before

Unfortunately, a beam similar to the one in the living room effectively divides the bed into two. One of the repercussions of this is that the woman has trouble sleeping. The room is too small to move the bed away, so light material should be draped over it to minimize its negative effects.

The solidity of the chest of drawers was helping to promote stability, but getting rid of the feeling of stagnation and opening up the space seemed more vital. The dried roses have been removed and the chest moved to the second bedroom, to allow chi to flow freely.

The end of the bed having thus been left open and vulnerable, the stripes of the new bedcover serve now to delineate the end of the bed and support the couple. Its bold

Problems people experience that can be identified as coming from one particular room or may need to be adjusted throughout the home. This bedroom is a continuation of the earlier consultation begun in the living room on pages 96–99. Improvements in this room alone would not resolve the couple's relationship and well-being. The bedroom is in the Relationships (2) area of the apartment, which is significant as the couple are about to marry. But she does not sleep well, waking up feeling tired in the morning, while he feels drained because he works extremely long hours. So, while sleep problems will be the focus of the consultation, there are changes to be made here which will have an effect on other aspects of the couple's life too – both together and individually.

There are a number of aspects in the bedroom which are making it difficult for her to sleep well: most especially, feelings about the shift in her relationship are currently causing her a great deal of concern. And both partners feel stressed by the fact that they do not have enough time to themselves and that they would like to have some energy to be creative in areas that are unrelated to their work. Here, then, we will look specifically at Creativity (7), Relationships (2) and Wisdom (8), while a general readjustment will try to ensure that chi can move freely around the bedroom, for where the flow of energy is obstructed physically in a space, it makes it much harder to flow in the aspect of life that it reflects.

**After**

One of two bedrooms in the apartment, this is a small room with just enough space for a double bed and wardrobe. Yet although the bedroom is small, it does not feel very cosy or nurturing as there is a great deal of white (walls, bedcover and pillows) which makes the room feel harsh. The second of the two sleeping areas is far too small to be thought of in terms of a true bedroom, so it is probably better to designate it as a dressing room and use it effectively, creating more useful storage space that will help to relieve some of the pressure in the main bedroom and living area.

There is a huge chest at the end of the bed blocking the room and making it very difficult to get around to the other side of the bed. This heavy piece of furniture makes the room feel too crowded and the chi cannot flow easily, and it is also sitting in the area of Creativity in the bedroom. Likewise, there is a bouquet of dried roses on the windowsill, which is in the area of the apartment associated with Creativity, an aspect of her life that she feels has also dried up at the moment. She needs clarity and direction to help her focus on a new future and find her way with a new career. There are two Impressionist oil paintings behind the bed, which represent indistinct images, and in the room's Relationships area there is a pencil sketch of a sad, grey-faced girl with downcast eyes – hardly inspiring as the first images that can be seen from the bed when waking in the morning.

**orange and gold stripes also brighten up the atmosphere, the stimulating red tones helping the occupants to feel more positive, particularly about relationships. She could have painted the walls a soft, light pink, but this might have been deemed too feminine. The harshness of a wrought-iron bedside table has been softened by a cloth, for a more nurturing atmosphere.**

**The rectangular mirror opposite the end of the bed, hung above the chest of drawers, was very bad for quality sleep. In its place, the colourful painting of people walking along a path through a field of wild flowers is a significant improvement. In addition, the painting of a pair of pretty flowers is much better than the rather sad picture of the girl.**

## TIPS FOR BEDROOMS

• Position your bed carefully so that you do not sleep directly in line with the door; you will be lying right in the path of energy coming into the room. Have a clear view of the door, and choose a solid wall behind you rather than an open area or a window.

• Try to avoid placing a bed under a beam or an overhanging built-in cupboard.

• Always have a headboard for support. Round wood or cloth headboards are best.

• If your back is to the door, place a mirror on the wall opposite, positioned to allow you to see anyone entering the room.

• Restrict mirrors to just one; choose a circular shape as it symbolizes energies being blended together.

• Avoid metal-framed beds which amplify the electro-magnetic radiation from other electrical equipment in the house.

• Choose natural fabrics for sheets and pillowcases whenever you can.

• Replace mattresses every six or seven years – sooner, if you undertake a new, important relationship.

• Keep anything work-related out of your bedroom – distractions too. Bedside books should be limited to one or two.

• Avoid overhead lights; for soft, relaxing light, use full-spectrum lighting in all lamps.

**ABOVE** Ceiling beams are a common problem, both in old houses and in newer homes where a feeling of authenticity is deemed paramount. In fact, they have a very detrimental effect on the quality of your sleep. The canopy here minimizes the beams' effect; it acts as a protective cover for the bed's occupants while they sleep and ensures that the energy above them moves smoothly, and the green fabric is well chosen because it is an uplifting colour. Historically, people slept in wooden-framed beds which contained their energy as they slept; a long stool here serves the same function. Rugs would be a happy addition; stone can feel cold in a bedroom.

**RIGHT** A wonderful sanctuary in a large bedroom – a place to retreat and read in the glow of a setting sun. Large, soft cushions, voluminous drapes, fresh flowers and a candle all contribute to the calm.

Although there are no hard and fast rules, people who find it difficult to settle at night should try to sleep in bedrooms which look west; rooms facing the sunrise in the east are ideal for elderly people and for those who find it hard to wake up. South-facing rooms – with the full energy of the sun all day – can be too stimulating, while those facing north may lack energy. See how you feel; make adjustments with warmer or cooler colours on the walls.

**ABOVE** Soft shades, simple furnishings and humble surroundings give this room a very restful feel, in contrast to the bright sunshine coming through the window, but without being too sparse. Whereas in a living room, a chair or side table might be used to display an ornament, furniture in a bedroom should always serve a function; otherwise it is better placed elsewhere. Smaller rooms are easier to transform into private retreats as they feel cosier, and their size often prevents them from becoming the focus of activity. Relaxation requires soft, gentle lines and shapes; art and ornament that is sharp, angular or disquieting should be discarded.

In the West, the colour white is associated with cleansing and thus it is a good colour for bathrooms. It will need warming up, however, with accents of colours such as green, peach, red or pink. A red towel is especially uplifting if the toilet is positioned in the area of Illumination (9). Here there are just a couple of pieces of red glass to introduce a warm touch.

While the uninterrupted simplicity of one colour is beneficial, there is also a richness and variety of texture in the room – with ceramics, wicker, wood, glass and cotton. There is also a good combination of flowing and straight lines, circles and squares, and few sharp angles.

The black-and-white diamond floor pattern is very powerful and a good way of holding the energy in a room where it is constantly and inevitably being drained by the downward pull of the plumbing. Plants would help to redress the energy imbalance here, while sea salt added to the bath would stop the drain of minerals from your body.

The huge oval mirror with its ornate – but white – frame not only opens up the space but helps all those who use this room to have a much greater sense of self.

# BATHROOMS

*The bathroom is a private space where we should feel relaxed as we unwind before bed, and squeaky clean and ready to brave anything at the start of the day. It must function efficiently as it is associated with personal internal plumbing and finances.*

Bathrooms are places for cleansing and purification and, as such, they need good lighting and ventilation, minimum clutter and privacy. They should be clean, airy and simple. It is in the bathroom that we are in communion with ourselves late at night before going to bed and first thing in the morning when we wake up. But bathrooms also represent waste; ideally they should be kept as far away from the kitchen as possible.

Modern houses are built with an ever-increasing number of bathrooms and toilets. Although this is usually seen as an advantage, in fact it puts too much downward energy into a house. And the positive energy which is flowing around a house will actively gravitate to toilets and drains and be sucked down them – the greater the number of outlets for water to flush through, the easier it is for energy to just drain away. As the movement of water is associated with wealth, so the number of toilets and the condition of the plumbing in a home will affect its occupants' financial condition. Having lots of plants where there is an excess of water energy will redress the balance, and to contain this energy it is good practice to keep the toilet seat down. Furthermore, to encourage the energy to circulate in the room, position the toilet as far away as possible from the door – but preferably not opposite the doorway.

When you wake up in the morning your body is at its most contracted because your energy has spent the whole night settling down. You should have things in your bathroom that make you chuckle or smile as laughter makes your body shake out. And a big mirror will prompt you to stretch, expanding your energy right to the extremities of your body. So, if you have the space, make the mirror really tall and wide, so that your reflection is as large and complete and clear as possible. Avoid storage cabinets with a divided mirrored front that splits your image in half, and also mirrors that are too low and too small. If you cannot see at least 20cm (8in) above your head, you will also reduce your potential because the image you see of yourself will be limiting.

A small bathroom will make you think more intensely about your body: bright lighting and big mirrors will create an illusion of space and encourage you to stretch and expand your horizons.

The walls above the blue tiles in this bathroom were a greyish off-white colour which made the room very stark. Bathrooms need to be bright and cheerful so the walls have been painted a bright green.

The blue tiles serve to magnify the water energy in a room, which already has a great deal of water, so introducing green, which symbolizes tree energy, helps to drain off some of the excess. Green is also a colour that is associated with money, so it will help the occupant's finances.

Even after the walls have been painted there is still an overwhelmingly large expanse of blue which makes the room feel quite cold. It can be warmed up, either by adding touches of red in the decor or by choosing towels in warm shades.

The original mirror above the basin was not very large. Although the occupant is not particularly keen to see more of himself, he does look into this mirror every day, and its size will have been restricting his sense of self and his ability to attract bigger projects. A bigger expansive mirror has been brought in to replace the little one in order to let him expand his potential. This change was particularly important because there are no other mirrors in the apartment.

In an otherwise very minimalist apartment, it might come as a surprise to find that the shelf above the basin in the bathroom was cluttered with toiletries – except that this clutter was standing between him and his reflection, which, in effect, is another block on his potential. Practically the busiest spot in the apartment, this shelf needed to be streamlined, as it is looked at every day; some of the items have been removed to a side table.

This apartment has been occupied by an artist for the last seven years. He has arranged the space unusually, converting one room into a studio and having very little furniture in the large space which is the main living room where he displays art that he finds inspiring. Although he is very successful, he is keen to develop his career and take on larger commissions; while he is a very private person, not eager to put himself in the spotlight, he would like his work to become better known. He earns enough from year to year, but cash flow is irregular which means that he has anxieties about finances.

The owner has been trying to open up the space in his living room which will help to nourish the energy in Wisdom (8) and make him feel less anxious. Significantly, however, his first comment about his apartment was an instruction on how to flush the toilet, for it needs a few flushes before the water comes in. Making the bathroom the focus of this consultation, we can address the areas of the bagua which reflect his concerns: Fortunate Blessings (4) and Illumination (9).

**Before**

After

Before

The flow of life-enhancing water is symbolically linked to the flow of wealth and opportunities, so any problems that you might have with your plumbing are going to have a direct impact on your bank account. The water flow into the toilet is slow, which indeed mirrors the financial situation, where money comes in inconsistently and too slowly. The fact that the plumbing needs attention reflects an inability to attract and save money. His priority, even after these changes, must be to call in a plumber.

After

The inevitable flow of water – and energy – down the toilet bowl, which tends to have an adverse effect on finances, is aggravated here because the toilet is situated in the area of Fortunate Blessings (4), which is usually associated with wealth. A strong, upward-growing plant has been placed on the shelf to use up some of the excess water energy, its bright yellow pot with gold trim chosen because bright colours and reflective metal hold energy and uplift it. The air vent above, originally hidden by a rather grey painting, has been uncovered and painted green.

The window is in the Illumination (9) area of the bathroom, a good place to work on the occupant's reputation. The windowsill was cluttered with toiletries but it has been tidied up and more fire energy introduced: a candle and a red plant in a green pot, and a beautiful red card to stimulate fire energy. A faceted crystal could also be hung in the window. The picture above the bath represents a project in which the occupant would like to be involved; looking at it every day will make it more achievable.

The dark brown window blind was kept rolled up to let as much light into the room as possible, only bringing it down at night to keep in warmth. A blind in translucent apple green fabric, tied with blue ribbons, has been installed to make this area brighter.

Bathrooms need to be brightly lit. On the contrary, this bathroom was lit by a low-wattage bulb, diffused by an old, dim shade. It needed to be replaced with a more powerful bulb in a white glass globe. The lampshade could even carry a metallic pattern in gold or silver, which would help to activate energy every morning.

## TIPS FOR BATHROOMS

• Bathrooms can be located anywhere in the home but given the choice, avoid anywhere near the front door, in Fortunate Blessings (4), or the centre of the house. If that is not possible, corrective measures include putting plants that grow upright around the toilet, keeping the lid down and hanging a small convex mirror on the outside of the door to prevent energy going in and being lost. Chi energy is most active at the front of the house so if it is to be lost, it is better for it to be lost from the back of the house where it has less force.

• If the toilet is next to the kitchen, hang a ceramic mobile (associated with soil energy) between the two rooms to moderate the balance of the different energies.

• Ensure that all the plumbing functions properly – no leaks, or faults with the infill, or noises. A steadily dripping tap, however slow, indicates an erosion of your finances.

• Your internal plumbing will reflect the health of your bathroom too. If you do have problems physically, make sure you sort them out along with the home's waterworks.

• Keep the room warm; avoid triangles, sharp edges and corners, and cold or hard metallic materials. Alone or in combination, they will make you feel very uncomfortable when you are undressed.

• Have your bath or shower installed next to a wall if possible, rather than a window which would make you feel insecure.

**LEFT** It is crucial to incorporate items in the bathroom that will counteract the draining effect of the plumbing on the room's energy. The tall plant in the reed basket provides strong upward energy. The plant also acts as a screen between the mirrors which are facing each other, thereby preventing the reflection of the bather from disappearing as it continues into infinity. Windows are important for ventilation but are generally better away from the bath, although here the blind can be drawn to enclose the space.

**BELOW** The square tiles in this very modern bathroom give it a very masculine feel and the flow of energy is conducive to money-making. Having two sinks means that more water is flowing into the room – financially good – and the tree energy of the counter is an effective way of soaking up the water energy that is flowing out down the drains. Extending across both sinks and, crucially, without a join in the centre, the large mirror is excellent, its size likely to prompt a good stretch in the morning.

**LEFT** If the bathroom has no window onto the outside world, create the illusion of more space by hanging a mirror on the wall, or a photograph or painting of something natural. Choose an image characterized by upward movement to counter the natural movement of energy in this room, which is always downward: the checks of the towels here will act as a control. The potentially negative angularity of the ceiling space has been softened by using it to store towels. And the softness of the hanging towels is very positive because it will make you feel cosy and secure while you are standing in the space where you are most likely to feel vulnerable, usually in a state of undress.

# CHILDREN'S ROOMS

*Children seem to know intuitively what is good for them. Their rooms should be simple and cosy, filled with symbols of possibility and imagination, somewhere where it is possible to develop a sense of self as well as having enough space to play.*

Children change fast as they grow up; they seem different from month to month. Obviously, they need their surroundings to reflect this momentum so you should be prepared to change the colour scheme and the way the furniture is arranged at least every two years. Watch to see if a child adjusts where he or she sleeps in a bed or if they physically move during the night and wake up somewhere else in the room. If they do not sleep well, check that there is nothing stored under their bed or hanging over it. Let them choose how they want the room decorated rather than dictating your preferred colour scheme; they need to feel that they have some control of their space and it does prepare them for decision-making later in life. It is important to ensure that a child's room has a focal point: a mobile by a window, or a special place for certificates. A clock is good, too, particularly one with a second hand; its constant presence helps to encourage a child to develop a better sense of time-keeping.

Choose a square or rectangular room for a child, rather than anything irregular in shape. When you decorate the room, do not add moulding to split the wall in half horizontally as this sets limits in the children's surroundings – the opposite of what you want alongside their growing and developing personalities. Nor should you constrain them with stripes and squares, and try to avoid frightening and aggressive images which are not conducive to feelings of safety and security.

Bright, primary colours are great fun and generally ideal for play areas, although they may over-stimulate some very active children, but it is probably better to avoid red in a bedroom; the colour of energizing fire energy, it is hardly appropriate. Similarly, busily patterned wallpaper or jazzy wall coverings are too stimulating and should be changed. Generally speaking, softer, paler colours are best; with a more neutral background on the wall you can moderate the amount of stimulation you feel your child might need by experimenting with different bedcovers, toys and posters. Green is soothing as well, but cooling colours like blue may be *too* sedating, particularly if the room has little light and is north-facing. Of course, colours affect different children in different ways, so you need to watch what happens when you make changes.

This room is simple and open, dominated by an incredibly beautiful fantasy tree painted on the wall. The tree energy obviously generated by the painting is a good way to lift a corner like this, where the bed has been placed under a slightly sloping ceiling. The wooden headboard also lends further support. Trees are symbols of growth, so this will also act as a powerful stimulant for the occupant to develop powers of creativity and resourcefulness. It will also encourage independence and inner strength as the child will be less dependent on toys and external influences. The uncluttered nature of the room and the small library by the side of the bed suggests that the child who lives here loves stories. There is only one soft toy even visible, so he or she must be very self-reliant.

Whenever possible, it is better to give children of different ages separate rooms; if they have to share, screens can be used to divide a larger room to give them privacy and allow them to develop more self-reliance and self-esteem. Above all, allow children to personalize their space. Balance is the key: give them the freedom to be creative, but give them security too.

**Before**

The most important thing to change in this room was the position of the bed. It needed to be moved as much as possible from underneath the eave, and from behind the door. Although small children often like to sleep in enclosed spaces, in fact this is not good for their long-term development.

The bed has been turned so that he sleeps with his head to the other wall; not only will he have a good view of the door,

The young occupant of this bedroom is nine years old and lives with his parents in the last of a row of houses. He does not generally sleep very well and this situation has not improved since the family recently moved into this particular house from a small, cramped apartment. The bedroom is one of two rooms on the second storey at the top of the house, both of them under the eaves; it is a converted attic with sloping ceilings. His bed is currently positioned under one of those eaves and he sleeps with the back of his head to the door on a bed without a headboard. He is likely to outgrow this room in a couple of years, but his parents intend to have moved on by then anyway.

The room is a typical child's room with a collection of several cuddly toys and posters of favourite sports heroes stuck to the walls and sloping ceiling. The shelving

**Before**

unit holds the boy's own television set for his computer games and there is a fishtank above it. The tank has an electric filter pumping the water and therefore makes a constant whirring noise.

While the boy loves sports, and seems to be doing well in this area, the school he attends is very academic and he has been finding it quite a struggle to keep up. He has recently been diagnosed as dyslexic and is now receiving some remedial tutoring to help him with his studies.

This consultation, in endeavouring to address the boy's sleep problems and learning difficulties, will focus on the room layout and colour rather than on changes to particular houses of the bagua of his room.

**but he is free from the acute pressure exerted by the pointed eave, the most likely cause of his sleeping difficulties. The posters on the ceiling would have been increasing this pressure, so these have also been removed. By adding a headboard to the bed, the effects of the ceiling above are lessened still further.**

**In addition, the whole room needed to be re-decorated as well. The walls and ceiling**

After

were painted bright yellow, with the woodwork in white. Small spaces like this need to be opened up and benefit from being painted one colour throughout. This will visually expand the space, diminish the joins in an angular room by making the many edges start to disappear, and reduce the emphasis on a sloping ceiling. Yellow is a strong gathering colour and is really far too intense for this small area.

Green has been chosen to replace the yellow, and the woodwork will be painted a similar colour later. The colour of nature, green is more healing and soothing than yellow. It symbolizes upward tree energy which is not only good for a loft space but also encourages growth. In the middle of the spectrum, it helps to synthesize the brain's two hemispheres and aid learning. This is supportive to dyslexic children.

Both duvet covers needed attention. Bold, coloured stripes have been replaced by softer checks in a colour that matches the walls. The other cover features a map of the world – far too expanding for most small children – and needs to be changed for something more reassuring. A storybook character would be more appropriate.

The green whale mobile that has been hung near the bed has created a good focal point in the room. The fishtank, however, has been removed. All electrical appliances in the home give off some electro-magnetic radiation, so it helps not to have any such equipment in bedrooms. If it is unavoidable, it should at least be switched off at the mains or unplugged when not in use. With its motorized pump bubbling noisily all night, the tank is almost bound to have been partly responsible for the boy's sleeping

After

problems. Plants help to cleanse the air and neutralize the effects, so a plant has been placed next to the television.

Two favourite toys have been selected to sit on his bed. All children need guardians and deep within our psyche we are aware of what all animals symbolize: thus the fox is reputedly clever, intelligent and a quick thinker – a great support for his studies.

The posters of people on the sloping eaves accentuate the downward pressure. These can be transferred to a straight wall.

A general clear-out with mother was called for so that her possessions would be more current. Childish books needed to be passed on or put away in the basement and room made for the more grown-up books that she will read. The bookcases were extremely cluttered and these have now been pared down. In time, it would be a good idea to build doors over the corner shelf area to make a cabinet to screen off and hide all the books.

The bed has been moved from having its back in the corner of the room so that the girl's head is now fully against the wall. Having her head facing into an angle was not good because the energy around her head was being dissected by the sharp corner pointing towards her. The bed now is flat against the back wall and a small space has been left to allow some walking space on both sides. A glimpse in the mirror now placed above the fireplace shows when people are entering the room. The droopy plant on the mantelpiece has been taken away and another, which grows upwards, has been put on the sideboard.

The rocking horse sitting in the doorway represented masculine energy and acted like a protective guardian, but it belongs more comfortably in the rooms of children of nursery school age. The horse has been moved out of the room into storage in the basement. A poster can now be placed on the wall behind the horse with an image of either a horse, a tree or a house. This would still act as a reassuring guardian image and help with the transition into teens. As it is in the area of Elders (3) in the room, it will also support her relationship with her parents as she grows older.

**Before**

The eleven-year-old girl who sleeps in this room is a youngster preparing to move from girlhood into her teens. She is an only child who lives with her parents in a detached, Victorian house and attends a local school. She is very much in a transitional phase at the moment, as her room testifies – with posters of pop stars and grown-up nail polishes alongside a collection of very precious fluffy toys and dolls.

She is a very happy and well-balanced child with no health problems or difficulties at school. The priority for the consultation in her room will be to support her in this transitional period as she moves through her teens into womanhood. This can be a very traumatic time and she will need the strong support of both parents, but particularly her mother, while at the same time trying to carve out her own way in the world. The suggested changes will focus on how to achieve this transition smoothly.

She has quite a large room with the bed angled into the corner, with its back to the wall by the door. The ceiling is high but our attention is brought down by a wallpaper border featuring pink roses, and the plain, pale pink walls serve as a good, clear backdrop to all the pictures and posters. The room feels generally cluttered with quite a strong horizontal bias. The dressing-table mirror is half obscured by a collection of necklaces and scarves and the tabletop is bursting with jewel boxes and toiletries. Dominating the entire space, however, is a beautiful wooden rocking horse that the occupant has had since she was a baby.

Before

Currently in the Elders (3) area are pin-up posters of rock stars; these should be transferred to Creativity (7), around the mirror. The pictures that were hanging unevenly from the picture rail, obscuring the border paper, have been rehung lower on the wall.

The floral border was quite busy and old-fashioned, and not well liked. It has been replaced with a more structured and more modern flower pattern that she chose herself, which will help her to be more focused. It actually features all five colours of the five moving energies cycle, so it adds a good balance to the room.

The bed has a new blue bedcover – a calming colour – with a pretty strawberry pattern drawing red stripes to add direction in the occupant's life. A round bedside table with a lamp has been introduced.

The mirror by the door has been hung on the wall but it will need adjusting so that she has a good, unrestricted view of herself and a good 20cm (8in) of space above her head.

After

Soft toys have been placed in the dark fire grate which had previously been blocked by a picture leaning against it.

The large collection of quartz crystals that was next to the bed on a square antique chair has been moved, because the crystals would magnify any negativity in the room. They do need to be cleaned regularly, but can be displayed elsewhere.

The dressing table has been cleared and the top of the mirror uncovered. The new yellow gingham bows and blue frills are far more grown-up than the pink ones they have replaced.

After

### TIPS FOR CHILDREN'S ROOMS

• Children's rooms should be simple and cosy and filled with symbols of possibility and imagination. Avoid abstract images that are too complex for younger children.

• Increase a child's sense of security by positioning the bed so that the child can see the door when in it.

• Give them a bedside light or main light switch so that they feel more in control about choosing when they want to read without getting out of bed.

• Place a mirror somewhere away from the bed, tall enough for a child to see his or her full height and a bit more. This helps them to develop a strong sense of self. Keep moving the mirror up or buy a larger one.

• Keep the room clean; help children to keep order without being too rigid. This will increase their vitality and energy.

• Choose furniture and shelving with curved lines as this will help children to grow creatively and remain flexible.

• As well as a sleeping area, try to plan to have enough floor space to play on.

• Whenever possible, separate children of different ages to let them develop more self-reliance. Above all, give children privacy and allow them to personalize their space.

• Avoid bunk beds as one child will be cramped below, the other near the ceiling.

**RIGHT** Creativity is stimulated by the round lines of the stools and table, while the squareness in the blackboard and drawers will encourage some control and structure for thoughts. Images of animals should always be recognizable and friendly: young children find dogs reassuring. Bright colours here are really stimulating for young minds; it would be great if this were a separate room and not visible from the sleeping area.

**RIGHT** Watch how the decor of a room affects the personality of your child. This example would be perfect for a child needing discipline and order – with its square structure and square-patterned fabrics – and the neat storage and square furniture. It would be too much for a highly creative child who would find it restrictive, and blue is a very cool and introspective colour, although the yellow does warm it.

**LEFT** Although some children might find this mural frightening, these animals will be the perfect guardians if the room's occupants like them. To keep the area above their heads clear, the cotton canopies should be removed, unless they are actually used. The bedside table acts as a boundary between the children, while the matching beds will prompt a good relationship between them.

**RIGHT** The verticality of tall cupboards, shelf units and stripes helps to keep a child's energy growing upwards. A curtain is ideal for separating the play area from the bed.

When people can work from home there is much more opportunity to create uplifting environments which really support them. This room is an inspiring place to work, with its view out to the garden, the natural wooden floor, the bay tree and the large amount of space to display and store work in progress. The soft folds of the curtains and the curved wall allow the energy to move smoothly. It is a highly creative environment that, with the addition of the square desk as a focal point, allows that creativity to be turned into money. A square or rectangular room, with furniture characterized by right angles, is best for money management and decision-making (more logical left-brain functions) while curves, circles and ovals are better for stimulating creativity (more intuitive right-brain functions).

Taking advantage of the view means that the person sitting at the desk will have an exposed back but the shiny desk lamp will bear reflections of anyone moving behind them. And shiny metal picture frames, uplighting and a tall healthy plant combine to activate the Fortunate Blessings (4) corner of the room.

# WORK SPACES

*Working from home can give you a sense of freedom. You might not be able physically to leave the office behind and head for the sanctuary and shelter of your home, but you can create your own stress-free working environment.*

The nature of the workplace and business life is changing extremely fast. Advances in computer technology and international communications mean that people can work from anywhere: forecasters say that by the beginning of the twenty-first century, over half the population of North America will be working from home and that this trend will be quickly followed in Europe. This trend provides people who work for themselves, those who work from home and are linked to the office by computer, or freelancers with a great opportunity, discontinuing the need to travel to a central office.

This revolution is having a dramatic impact on our lives. Our homes are in danger of becoming frenetic nerve centres for our business activities. By using feng shui principles and an awareness of how the environment affects us, it is entirely possible to create living and working environments that will sustain us. The key is to achieve balance in how space will be used and to determine the boundaries, so that there is a way to shut the door and bring closure at the end of each working day.

The place you choose to have as your home office or study becomes a microcosm for the whole business. It is best to locate this room nearest to your front door, especially if you have visitors, as you do not want them walking through the family rooms; it also reinforces a stronger relationship with the outside world. Choose a quiet room, or at least keep the door closed, so that you take yourself away from the comings and goings of the home. Distractions will interrupt your train of thought.

The shape of the room and the contents will determine the focus of your energy. Everything must be well organized. The position of the desk is very important, as is the arrangement of the space, so that energy can flow easily. Place your desk so that you have a solid wall behind you rather than a window or open walkway and make sure that nothing with a sharp angle is pointing directly towards you. Do not have your desk at an angle across a corner and try to sit with a clear view of the door, but make sure that you are not sitting opposite it – right in the path of the energy coming into the room. Keep the wall area behind your desk plain so that people are not distracted by artwork or message boards while they are listening to you.

**Before**

The owner of this detached four-bedroomed house is an actor. He does not feel fortunate at the moment and describes his career as being in a 'go-slow' period. He says that success is missing from his life. Because he does not seem to attract enough good acting jobs, he feels financially challenged and consequently stressed. He cannot understand why his talents are not getting him the recognition and jobs he wants and feels he deserves.

The owner uses the spare bedroom as his study. Although most of his work takes him away on location, he does use the room more than he originally planned to. When he thought about his daily routine, he realized that, in fact, he does quite a lot of work from home. On those days when he is not out on an acting job, he makes networking telephone calls from home. He will also check in here every morning before he goes out to work. The room is actually the organizational foundation and focal point of his working life.

The room has an identity crisis. While the occupant calls it his 'study', he does get upset when other members of the family come in and move his possessions around. However, nobody seems to view the territory as 'off-limits', and his wife still refers to it as the 'spare room'.

This is not a very empowering environment and it is affecting the occupant's ability to be successful. Everybody needs a power base, a place from which to go out and conquer, and this is what needs to be created here. If you do not actually go into an office away from your home every day, it is important to set up a winning environment within your own space.

**After**

The first thing that could be seen from the doorway of the room was a large double bed with a white bedspread and old wooden frame. It stood in the centre of the room, dominating the space, and made it much harder to focus on work. Rarely used, and only then by occasional overnight guests, it has been replaced by a small sofa.

The walls are covered in a William Morris wallpaper featuring leaves and lemons. The occupant likes the wallpaper but it is very distracting. When he gets really used to working and concentrating in this room, he will begin to feel it crowding him. The room will then need to be repainted – a more neutral off-white or cream. This will create a simpler environment and will allow energy to be focused on the work in hand.

To the right, as you enter the room, is a washbasin set in a tiled area with a mirror above it. To remove all traces of this room having been a bedroom, a screen has been placed against the washbasin so that it cannot be seen. The same screen can be used to shield the desk if the room is ever used as a guest bedroom.

To the left as you go into the room was an old wardrobe with mirrored panels on the doors. This has been taken away because it is simply bedroom furniture being used to store junk and old work. The useful contents are now stored on a small shelf unit.

Around the rest of the room was a variety of wooden tables and shelves full of files of household accounts and folders of work. On one shelf, there were a number of family portraits. One desk had a computer on it, while current paperwork, a telephone, address file and lamp were on the other desk, positioned by the window.

After

**Before**

The desk has been moved; anyone sitting at it used to enjoy the view out of the window but it was distracting. Now it is positioned where the wardrobe used to be, in the Fortunate Blessings (4) area. Here there is the support of a solid wall, and the door can be seen, so it is in the power position. The view through the window can still be observed. A bigger and more attractive desk would be a sound investment, as it is difficult to build a strong career on second-hand equipment. Something more solid and supportive than the old typist's chair would be worthwhile too.

The occupant had to rethink what he needed on his tidy but cluttered desk. The telephone is now on a long cord so that it can move between the window chair and the desk. When on the desk, it should sit by his right elbow in Helpful Friends (6) as networking gets him most of his jobs.

A crystal hangs in the top right window to activate the chi coming into the room and to stimulate Fortunate Blessings; a crystal bowl placed in the same area on the desk will receive the flow of wealth, and a tiny, Oscar-like statue stands in the same area opposite his chair.

A relaxing chair has been placed in the bay window area with a small round table – an ideal place to be creative; he can choose to sit at the oblong desk when the work requires him to be entirely focused.

The Journey (1) area of the room has been sorted out: the filing given more breathing space, the display of pictures of his wife's relatives removed, and replaced by an inspirational movie poster.

Plants have been placed next to the computer on the side table and on the desk to counteract the negative influence of electro-magnetic energy.

This bedroom can be seen from the front door. It used to be a huge drawing room and is laid out as a study – though with many functions – with a bed lost in one corner. It is difficult to feel settled and contained in such a large area and with the desk and computer in the centre of the room, reminders of work are constant. Indeed, she has a clear view of her desk from her bed every night, symbolizing the lack of boundaries she has between her private life and her work, and making it very hard to switch off.

When you do have to use your bedroom as a study it is most important that you create distinct boundaries between work and rest. A more secure feeling has been created here by screening off the sleeping area. Arrange the space so that you do not notice the bed while you are working and cannot see the work area when you have finished. This helps to give a sense of completion to the working day.

There were piles of magazines, books and reports on the bedside table and on the floor at the end of the bed; the sideboard and desk were both piled high with work and the table had lots of compact discs. Having a good clear-out was important to help the occupant feel less overwhelmed. To have a mass of incomplete work and unread books and magazines as the last image at night and the first one on waking is a major cause of stress and affects the quality of sleep.

Eight prints of stern-looking Chinese scholars in the area of Wisdom (8) looked down disapprovingly on this woman, probably contributing to her constant internal dialogue. These have been replaced with two paintings of couples.

Before

This very elegant, one-bedroom city apartment has been occupied by a single professional woman for nine years. She has worked as an economist for seventeen years which she enjoys but dislikes the very long hours, the frenetic pressure of the job and the working environment where two hundred people struggle in a competitive, noisy, open-plan office. She says she feels trapped and unnourished. She is 'self-contained', as she puts it, and admits to having chosen many equally self-reliant friends. She is not in a relationship and would like to be; she referred to needing to feel more 'integrated' several times. However, she does not feel she has enough free time to do anything about this. And even when she tries to relax, she says she has a busy internal dialogue. She feels that money is too important in her life and worries a great deal about it rather than feeling blessed with what she has. This cumulative stress is affecting her physical well-being, and her exercise regime and commitment to healthy eating have lapsed.

While this woman feels creative in her work, she says creativity is missing from her personal life. She would like more time for herself. It is noticeable that the main artwork in the focal point of the living room is a montage of several pieces of other artwork, a disjointed image reinforcing her need to feel whole.

This consultation will help to establish a sense of serenity in her life and a healthier balance between work and time off. It will focus on the Journey (1) to open up her career, and Relationships (2) and Wisdom (8) because she is looking for a loving relationship and a better relationship with herself. To address these issues effectively, adjustments should be made in her study/bedroom.

After

**After** *above and left*

and has very tall ceilings and windows. Strong tree energy represents drive and ambition and is therefore not nurturing, so it needs to be drained by some fire: touches of red have been introduced, including the flowers in the dark fireplace. A heavier horizontal emphasis would also help.

Meanwhile, she has chosen to bring in a more vibrant image with a red and coral coloured urn to replace the stark, grey painting above the fireplace – a container from which her creativity can now pour.

Otherwise there are about fifty images of solitary figures in the apartment, the impact of which needs to be minimized, if this occupant's desire for a relationship is to be fulfilled. She needs to be surrounded by more images of twosomes, especially above the bed and in the Relationships (2) area.

The two empty birdcages on top of the wardrobe have been removed. In Fortunate Blessings (4) in both her bedroom and the apartment, they were inhibiting as they symbolized the emptiness of her life.

The room was dominated by a huge palm; it was taking over the space and rendered almost half the room unusable. The palm's massive fronds with their blade-like leaves were pointing right at the desk and would make sitting here extremely uncomfortable. To make better use of the room and remove the 'dagger-like' energy over the desk, the straggly leaves have been tied up to emphasize the height of the plant; two or three of the most intrusive lower leaves have been removed.

The desk itself is a trestle table which looks rather precarious and sat in the centre of the room with its back to the door. This was an extremely insecure spot, and the occupant found that she did not sit there; instead she gravitated to the dining table in the main living room. The desk has been moved so that she can now sit facing the door, her back supported by the wood panelling by the window. In time, she should replace the desk with something more solid.

The apartment has a tremendous amount of tree energy as many things are made of wood – furniture, panelling and shutters –

**Before**

## TIPS FOR WORK SPACES

• With space likely to be short, good organization is vital. Keep the place tidy as a messy environment will disturb your ability to think clearly.

• Try to create two different energies in the room: one bright for active and outward work and the other soft and receptive for study, where you can concentrate.

• Office electrical equipment causes much indoor pollution and electro-magnetic radiation. To disperse these discharges, which cause tiredness and stress, ensure there is good ventilation; employ an ionizer to boost negative ions, and use natural materials rather than plastics.

• Balance the electro-magnetic discharges with living things. Some plants cleanse the atmosphere – spider plants, poinsettias and jade plants. Place at least one next to each piece of electrical equipment.

• The ideal desk should combine square and round shapes; a square area with your files and computer and a creative circular area.

• Work on the horizontal or you will feel overwhelmed by large piles of things to do.

• Make sure everything works, and fix anything as soon as it breaks down.

• Keep the room fresh and remove waste daily, rather than letting stagnation build up. And be sure that you can close off the work space at the end of the day.

**LEFT** The square tables, shelves, boxes, window and blind, and square pattern in the chairs, make this a good learning environment, right for a student of sciences rather than art. The chairs give good support and will encourage the student to linger while, being metal, the chairs and desk frames help focused thinking and concentration. Be mindful of the power of symbols when you select art or ornaments. Use them as positive reinforcements: the helicopter here can be considered a good symbol for a bird's-eye view, seeing the bigger picture of a situation.

**OPPOSITE** This work area has a good combination of wood, which stimulates creativity, and metal, which helps people to focus. This is a good place to organize and finalize the creative process. The desks are all on wheels which is good for teamwork and for changing the office layout for the changing needs of the business. However, as they are movable, it would be better to have the floor one solid colour to provide a more solid foundation. Green plants are also needed to balance the electrical equipment.

**LEFT** The beautiful classical curves of this desk make it very inviting. The elaborate carvings add a sense of precision which will help the writer to concentrate. The mirror expands the space so the person is not facing a blank wall and can see what is going on behind him or her. The creatively sinuous lamp and curves make this an inspirational place for letter-writing while the squareness that characterizes the mirror makes it an efficient area as well.

# CONCLUSION

*ABOVE  Choose artwork that you feel connected to or which symbolizes something important for you. Art displays the state and depth of your spirit so don't just use it to avoid empty walls. Make it meaningful as you will see it every day.*

*RIGHT  Where rooms have two functions, arrange them to suit both purposes. If your kitchen is also a dining room, it is important to make the actual cooking process recede while you eat. Clear away all signs of preparation when the meal is ready and create a different ambience with low lighting around the table and darkness in the kitchen.*

### Take care, do it gradually

Before you start changing your environment, I will reiterate the importance of clearing out first. Adding an enhancement like a mirror to correct negative space will not do any good if the room is cluttered. You will only amplify any difficulties in your life, quite simply doubling your troubles. So be ruthless in your home and only keep the items which have a purpose or which you love. You will find that the clearer your environment, the more clarity there will be in your life and the more space there will be for opportunities to come your way. When you do make changes, take it step-by-step so that you can check what works and what doesn't. You may find strange coincidences happening – a plant placed with strong intention for family harmony one day could precipitate a phone call from an estranged relative the next morning. Watch for these happenings, keep making the changes and observe the results, which may not be visible immediately. If nothing happens after a calendar month, try another solution. However, if you go through your house like a tornado in one weekend and change the whole landscape then expect a whirlwind to pass though your life! Take it gradually.

### Your own personal energy is important

There are many factors affecting your own levels of personal energy. These include your diet, lifestyle and whether you exercise; the constitution inherited from your parents; your personality, upbringing and physical characteristics largely determined by your astrological profile set when you were born; other people around you and events out of your control; plus your surroundings. As much as your physical environment will have an effect, you can transcend it if your personal energy is strong. There are certainly difficult houses, those built with a challenging shape without any thought to creating harmony for the occupants and with more priority for satisfying financial constraints than aesthetics, which will be harmful. While there is no question that we are products of our environment, it is possible to rise above all these influences. The key is to have strong personal energy. To achieve this it is important to eat well, pay attention to where we prepare our food, sleep well and keep our homes as clear and natural as possible. If we can do that, difficult homes, traumatizing events and awkward people with whom we have to work will have less effect on us.

### Many different systems but all going to the same place

As your interest in this subject deepens, you will read books which will present many different systems. It is likely that you will find conflicting advice and become confused. The simplest solution is to stick with one system and master that before trying any

*ABOVE  Water placed in your environment acts as a powerful symbol of wealth and opportunities flowing into your life. This is important if you live in a built-up area without a garden or in a city with limited access to streams or rivers. Ensure that water placements stay fresh, either with movement or by changing daily. Fish add movement to water so they further activate the positive potential in the placement of water in your area of Fortunate Blessings (4). The fish placement in this picture would benefit from being in a larger, aerated tank.*

*Use water to refresh the atmosphere of rooms. You can do this by wiping down the surfaces in your office each morning to counter the negative effects of the electrical equipment, and you can introduce water through vases of flowers, thirsty plants and fishtanks.*

others. Feng shui is a deep, complex body of knowledge but at the end of the day you will find the various forms of feng shui are like spokes of a wheel which eventually all come together in one place. As you learn more you will see how the universal principles described in this book underpin the practise of feng shui and how the seemingly disparate strands weave together in a complex and beautifully intricate web.

### The creation of a sanctuary space is a must for revitalization

More and more people are retreating into their homes to escape the stresses of modern life, be they images of aggression in the world as seen in the newspapers, or heavier workloads and job insecurity. The answering machine, once a tool for taking messages while we were out, is now used to screen the calls from even our nearest and dearest when we are in! If we are to be able to cope effectively with what goes on around us which is out of our control, then it is vital that the homes we retreat to are set up to nourish us completely. Scientific evidence now proves the connection between mind and body, that high and consistent levels of stress will impair our immune systems and diminish our ability to cope. By understanding which elements in our environment actually add to the tension and by bringing in those elements which help to rebalance us and create our homes as sanctuaries, we are doing much to safeguard our health.

### Make your home a truly inspirational place

Feng shui can also help us to make our homes into personal places of power. Once you take on board the notion that your environment is simply a mirror for your life, then take a good look around you and decide if you like what you see. If you don't like it, change it – it really is as simple as that. If, for example, you are trapped in a job which is not letting you spread your wings and feel you are capable of much more but there is nothing on the horizon, it could be that you are living in a very small, cramped home. Instead of accepting that is all you can afford and feeling in a catch-22 situation – no opportunity, no money, therefore no room to manoeuvre – shift the energy in your home. Create a sense of space with whatever you have got. Remove non-essential furniture or belongings, lighten the colour schemes or add large mirrors to expand the rooms, bring in more living energy with plants and open up your vistas with posters of seascapes, mountains and horizons. All it takes is just a little effort invested in the right direction with the aim of transforming your environment so it supports your spirit.

### The key to interior design is inside you

Feng shui is very personal. It is your relationship with the space you live in, which is truly a reflection of you. It is virtually impossible to make any sensible feng shui adjustments for an empty home. Who will live there? What do they want? The real issue in feng shui is your ability to live by the principle 'as without so within'. The interior design of your home will determine the pattern and movement of chi just like your own internal patterns will determine your behaviour, attitude and actions. The reason you choose something which is not totally supportive is because at some level it resonates with a pattern inside you. Deep, long-lasting change can only come when we recognize this and pay attention to our inner bagua. Any transformation of your consciousness will be reflected into your external world. Real harmony at home will be achieved when we begin to design our lives from the inside out.

## Workplaces – adjust your home, then attend to your workplace

The environments in which some people spend a third of their lives obviously have an impact on their health and motivation. Although you may not have the authority or influence to make significant changes, do what you can. First of all, ensure that your home is supportive to you; protect your own energy with a good diet so that you can are less affected by difficult environments; and create an optimum environment in your working area. Set an example to others by making your space as joyful, natural and uplifting as you can. Bring in your own plants and pictures. Change can be so much more effective if is started at the bottom because the only way for it to go is up.

*BELOW Every home needs a place of sanctuary and retreat. This could be a private corner of your bedroom or a secluded area of your living room. It needs to feel inviting so that it draws you in, beckoning you at the end of a busy day. Surround yourself with comfortable and favourite things and each time you sit there, you will feel at peace as the surroundings become habitual, giving your mind and body familiar instructions to relax.*

# INFORMATION

# INDEX

## BIBLIOGRAPHY

### For a further understanding of placement

• *Feng Shui Made Easy* by William Spear, Thorsons
• *The Feng Shui Handbook* by Master Lam, Gaia
• *Healing Homes* by Dennis Fairchild, (available from PO Box 1781, Birmingham, Michigan 48012-1781)
• *The Western Guide to Feng Shui* by Kathryn Terah Collins, Hay House Inc.
• *Interior Design with Feng Shui* by Sarah Rossbach, Rider
• *The Feng Shui Book of Cures* by Nancilee Wydra, Contemporary Books
• *Feng Shui* by Angel Thompson, Picador
• *Home Design from the Inside Out* by Robin Lennox, Penguin Arkana

### For understanding more about the five energies

• *The Feng Shui Handbook* by Derek Walters, Thorsons
• *Practical Feng Shui* by Simon Brown, Thorsons
• *The Complete Illustrated Guide to Feng Shui* by Lillian Too, Element

### For understanding the time dimension

• *Feng Shui Astrology* by Jon Sandifer, Piatkus Books
• *The Principles of Feng Shui* by Simon Brown, Thorsons
• *The Ki - An Ancient Oracle for Modern Times* by Takashi Yoshikawa, Aquarian Press

### For practical support in clutter clearing

• *Clear Your Desk!* by Declan Treacy, Rider
• *Simplicity* by Elaine St James, Thorsons

### Towards a more natural way of living

• *The New Natural House Book* by David Pearson, Conran Octopus
• *The Natural Year* by Jane Alexander, Bantam Books
• *The Green Home* by Karen Christensen, Piatkus Books
• *Places of the Soul* by Christopher Day, Aquarian

### Learning more about cleansing homes and harmful energies

• *Creating Sacred Space with Feng Shui* by Karen Kingston, Piatkus Books
• *Sacred Space* by Denise Linn, Rider
• *Are you Sleeping in a Safe Place?* by Rolf Gordon, Dulwich Health Authority
• *Living with Electricity* by Powerwatch

### Learning more about ancient wisdom

• *The I Ching* translation by Richard Wilhem, Shambhala
• *The I Ching* translation by Master Ng, Shambhala
• *Signposts* by Denise Linn, Rider
• *The Wisdom of the Wyrd* by Brian Bates, Rider

### As within so without - improving your health and energy

• *Your Face Never Lies* by Michio Kushi, Avery Publishing Group
• *Sugar Blues* by William Dufty, Warner Books Inc.
• *The Self-Healing Cookbook* by Kristina Turner, Earth Stones Press
• *Food and Healing* by Annmarie Colbin, Ballantine
• *The Macrobiotic Way* by Michio Kushi, Avery Publishing Group
• *Food Governs Your Destiny* by Michio and Aveline Kushi, Japan Publications Inc
• *Psychic Protection* by William Bloom, Piatkus Books

## FENG SHUI NETWORK

For information on feng shui courses; consultations for homes and businesses with professional feng shui practitioners, space clearers and dowsers; speakers; professional training; purchasing these recommended books and others, videos and audio cassettes by mail order, contact:

Feng Shui Network International (FSNI)
PO Box 9, Pateley Bridge,
Yorkshire Dales,
HG3 5XG, England
Tel: +44 (0) 7000 336474
Fax: +44 (0) 1423 712869
Email: Feng1@aol.com.
Website: FengShuiNet.com
Gina Lazenby can be contacted via the above office.

# ACKNOWLEDGMENTS

## AUTHOR'S THANKS

A huge thank you to William Spear who was one of the key catalysts in my making a radical career change. After attending his course a new life path opened up before me. I have deeply appreciated his loving support and wisdom. Without him this book would not have been possible and I thank him for his input and guidance. Thanks also to my friend and feng shui colleague, Jan Cisek, for his tremendous support, his wise contributions, clarity, humour and for being a real gift in my life.

I wish to acknowledge the many excellent teachers who have been so important in the development of FSNI. In particular, Karen Kingston, for being a pioneering spirit in this work. My gratitude also to Roger Green, Jon Sandifer, Simon Brown (and Dragana), Takashi Yoshikawa, William Bloom, Suzanne Harper, Richard Creightmore and Peter Dawkins.

Thanks to the students who have joined the FSNI courses and helped to create a move towards living healthier, happier lives; to my colleagues at FSNI for their incredible dedication, in particular to Joanne Sharpe and Wendy Konyn who provided the space for me to write this book, and to my assistant Hayley Dennison for her sense of humour and for keeping me organized; to all the FSNI volunteer staff who have created a supportive community; to the clients from whom I have learnt so much; to my dear friend Annie Bradwell whose encouragement and contributions were invaluable; to Dennis Fairchild for his long-distance friendship and encouragement; to William Dufty whose brilliant book made such an impact on my life and health; to the amazing team at Conran Octopus for their tremendous support and patience; to the many teachers I have met and the authors whose books I have read for the contribution they have made to the understanding of feng shui; and to Morel, for his loving inspirations and our beautiful home where we support each other in living by what we teach.

## STYLIST'S CREDITS

I would like to thank the following for their cooperation in photography:

Clifton Nurseries, Paperchase, The Room, Mulberry, Hector Finch, Fired Earth, Osborne & Little, Jerry's Home Store, The Holding Company, Oggetti, Malabar, Designer's Guild, The General Trading Company, Donghia, Crucial Trading, Simon Horn, Highly Sprung, Muji, Snap Dragon, Colefax & Fowler, Laura Ashley, Harkin, Recline & Sprawl, Belinda Coote. Thanks also to Cinead McTernan for her enthusiasm.

## PHOTO CREDITS

Conran Octopus thanks the following for permission to reproduce photographs: **1** Hotze Eisma (designer: Marcel Wolterink); **2-3** Alexander van Berge/Elle Wonen; **4-5** Simon Brown/H&G/Robert Harding Syndication; **6-7** Bild Der Frau/ Camera Press; **8** Deidi von Schaewen; **8-9** Lizzie Himmel; **14** Jim Ballard/Getty Images; **15** *above* Pat O'Hara/Getty Images; **15** *below* Marie-Pierre Morel/ MCM; **20-21** Pat O'Hara/Getty Images; **21** Marie Pierre Morel/MCM; **22** Robert Harding Picture Library; **22-23** John Hall; **25** *above* Robert Harding Picture Library; **25** *below* Fritz von der Schulenburg/ Interior Archive; **26** Robert Harding Picture Library; **26-27** Paul Ryan (Wolgang Joop)/International Interiors; **29** *left* The Stock Market; **29** *right* Gilles de Chabaneix/Catherine Ardouin/MCM; **30** *above* David Jeffrey/The Image Bank; **30** *below* Ianthe Ruthven (Hodgson House, New Hampshire); **33** *above* Charles Wackler/The Image Bank; **33** *below* Andre Martin/MCM; **34** Rob Crandall/Planet Earth Pictures; **34-35** Marie-Pierre Morel/Catherine Ardouin/ MCM; **36** Jody Dole/The Image Bank; **37** Jean-Francois Jaussaud; **38** C. Simon Sykes/Interior Archive; **39** Simon Upton/H&G/Robert Harding Picture Library; **42** Paul Ryan (Kim Haistater)/ International Interiors; **43** *below* Paul Ryan (John Saladino)/International Interiors; **44** *above* Christian Sarramon (Olivier Gagneres, Paris); **44** *below* Tim Beddow/ Interior Archive; **45** *left* Janos Grapow; **45** *above right* Bild Der Frau/Camera Press;

**45** *below right* Paul Ryan (Brookes Buston)/International Interiors **46** Chris Meads; **47** *above* Chris Drake/Country Homes & Interiors/Robert Harding Syndication; **47** *centre* Nadia Mackenzie; **47** *below* Gilles de Chabaneix/Marie Kalt/MCM; **49** *left* Tom Leighton/Country Homes & Interiors/Syndication; **49** *above right* Tom Leighton/H&G Syndication; **49** *below right* Deidi von Schaewen (Trapp)/World of Interiors; **50-51** Paul Ryan (Piet Boon)/International Interiors; **51** *above right* Christian Sarramon; **51** *below right* Ray Main; **52** *below left* Marie-Pierre Morel/Christine Puech/MCM; **52-53** Simon Brown (courtesy of Neal Street East); **54** *above* Paul Ryan (Jack Lenor Larsen)/International Interiors; **54** *below* Jacques Dirand/Interior Archive; **55** *above* Marie-Pierre Morel/Catherine Ardouin/ MCM; **55** *below* Simon Brown/Interior Archive; **56** *left* Fritz von der Schulenburg/ Interior Archive; **56** *right* Jacques Dirand/Interior Archive; **57** Tim Beddow/Interior Archive; **58** C. Simon Sykes/Interior Archive; **59** *above left* Simon Upton/Interior Archive; **59** *above right* Tim Beddow/Interior Archive; **59** *below* Simon Upton/Interior Archive; **60** *left* Henry Wilson/Interior Archive; **60-61** Fritz von der Schulenburg/Interior Archive; **62** *above* Wulf Brackrock; **62** *below* Paul Ryan (Kristiina Ratia)/ International Interiors; **64** *above left* Marie-Pierre Morel/Christine Puech/MCM; **64-65** Paul Ryan (J. Balasz)/International Interiors; **65** *right* Simon Upton/Interior Archive; **66** *above* Michael Crockett/ Elizabeth Whiting & Associates; **66** *below left* Fritz von der Schulenburg/Interior Archive; **66-67** Pieter Estersohn/Lacha Pelle (Representation); **68-69** Karl Dietrich-Buhler/Elizabeth Whiting & Associates; **69** Mark Darley/Esto; **70** *above left* Andreas von Einseidel/Country Homes & Interiors/Robert Harding Syndication **70** *below left* Andreas von Einseidel/Country Homes & Interiors/ Robert Harding Syndication; **70** *right* Ariadne/VNU/Holland; **71** Polly Wreford/ Country Homes & Interiors/Robert Harding Syndication; **72-73** Ted Yarwood; **73** *above* Paul Ryan (Sam Blount)/International Interiors; **73** *below* Simon Brown/Interior Archive; **74** *left*

Peter Aaron/Esto; **74** *above right* Richard Felber; **74** *below right* Ted Yarwood; **75** Thibault Jeanson (Didier Gomez, Paris)/Inside; **76** *above left* Alexander van Berge; **76** *above right* Paul Ryan (James Gager)/International Interiors; **76** *below* Paul Ryan (Charles Rutherford)/ International Interiors; **77** Marie Pierre Morel/MCM; **80-81** Scott Frances/Esto; **88** Jonathon Pilkington/Interior Archive; **89** *left* Jonathon Pilkington/Country Homes & Interiors/Robert Harding Syndication; **89** *right* The Stock Market; **90-91** Richard Felber; **100** *left* Thibault Jeanson (Maison Lawrence, USA)/Inside; **100-101** Richard Felber; **101** Wulf Brackrock; **102-103** Jan Baldwin/H&G/ Robert Harding Syndication; **108** *above* Marianne Majerus/Country Homes & Interiors/Robert Harding Syndication; **108** *below left* Geoffrey Frosh/H&G/ Robert Harding Syndication; **108** *below right* Brigitte/Camera Press; **109** Tim Beddow/Interior Archive; **110-111** Paul Warchol; **120-121** Eric Morin; **121** *above right* Tim Beddow/Interior Archive; **121** *below* Richard Felber; **122-123** Simon Upton (courtesy of Keith Skeel)/World of Interiors; **128** *below* Joshua Greene; **128-129** Schoner Wohnen/Camera Press; **129** *right* Schoner Wohnen/Camera Press; **130-131** Wayne Vincent (Lesley Saddington)/Interior Archive; **140** *above* Schoner Wohnen/Camera Press; **140-141** Fair Lady/Camera Press; **141** *above right* Living/Camera Press; **141** *below right* Schoner Wohnen/Camera Press; **142** Andreas von Einseidel/Elizabeth Whiting & Associates; **152** VT Wonen/VNU/ Holland; **153** *above* Bild Der Frau/Camera Press; **153** *below* C.Simon Sykes/Interior Archive; **154** Polly Wreford/H&G/Robert Harding Syndication; **155** Simon Upton (Anne Boyd)/Interior Archive; **156** Alexander Bailhache/Christine Puech/ MCM; **157** Joshua Greene.

All other photos by Bill Batten, specially commissioned by Conran Octopus.

Every effort has been made to trace the copyright holders. We apologize for any unintentional omission and would be pleased to insert an acknowledgment in subsequent editions.